The Shadow Behind You:
Ghost History? or Folklore?

By Aline Miller-Musson

© Copyright 2006 Aline Miller-Musson.
All rights reserved. No part of this publication may be reproduced, stored in a retrieval system, or transmitted, in any form or by any means, electronic, mechanical, photocopying, recording, or otherwise, without the written prior permission of the author.

Note for Librarians: A cataloguing record for this book is available from Library and Archives Canada at www.collectionscanada.ca/amicus/index-e.html
ISBN 1-4120-9859-9

Printed in Victoria, BC, Canada. Printed on paper with minimum 30% recycled fibre. Trafford's print shop runs on "green energy" from solar, wind and other environmentally-friendly power sources.

TRAFFORD
PUBLISHING
Offices in Canada, USA, Ireland and UK

Book sales for North America and international:
Trafford Publishing, 6E–2333 Government St.,
Victoria, BC V8T 4P4 CANADA
phone 250 383 6864 (toll-free 1 888 232 4444)
fax 250 383 6804; email to orders@trafford.com
Book sales in Europe:
Trafford Publishing (UK) Limited, 9 Park End Street, 2nd Floor
Oxford, UK OX1 1HH UNITED KINGDOM
phone 44 (0)1865 722 113 (local rate 0845 230 9601)
facsimile 44 (0)1865 722 868; info.uk@trafford.com
Order online at:
trafford.com/06-1615

10 9 8 7 6 5 4 3 2 1

TABLE OF CONTENTS

Acknowledgements	2
Prologue	4
Imagination? Or Fact?	6
St. Augustine, Oldest Town in the New World	11
Savannah, Shaped From the Wilderness	15
Educational Profiles	18
The Lost State of Franklin	20
Take a Ghost Tour and Let Your Imagination Run Free	22
Tour Groups Not Universally Loved	33
A New "Believer" in St. Augustine	36
Cemeteries – Fertile Ground for Ghost Stories	48
Perhaps Not All of the Cemetery Residents are Resting Quietly	57
Different Opinions – Different Stories	64
Some Noted Spirits in Savannah	69
Lots of Tales in Haunted Savannah	72
Hot Commodities: Ghosts, Bed & Breakfasts, and Inns	79
Hospitality Industry Brisk in St. Augustine	85
Haunted Inns Elsewhere	87
Ghost Community Active	91
Ghost Tour Guide Has Haunting Experiences	92
Other Places, Other Stories	97
Disbelievers Have Their Say	104
Reserved Opinions	108
Questions Remain	109

ACKNOWLEDGEMENTS

This has been an enjoyable and educational ride. I've had a lot of help and am grateful for all the assistance I've received in exploring the history, the tour attractions, and the world of the paranormal.

My warmest thanks to husband Ken Musson, who did much of the photography and assisted in computer technology to enable me to complete this document. He also used his former newspaper editing skills to help clean up the copy, and dug way back into his layout days by putting the finishing touches on the book material and making it into a book to be published. My thanks, also, for Ken's support and patience as my hours were sometimes eaten up by the computer in finishing "The Shadow Behind You."

I so appreciated the enthusiasm of David Saunders who shared his experiences and his photographs. His excited tale of his first "paranormal encounter" was refreshing and enjoyable.

My son, Barry Miller constantly encouraged me in my endeavor and shared a multitude of research data on the subject of the paranormal that he had gathered, as he traveled into cyberspace looking for clues about this new endeavor his mother was attempting. Although he was not a dedicated believer in the supernatural, he became a devoted fan of exploring the possibility that there is something out there that is unexplainable. He went sleuthing with his friend, Cynthia Tanner, to possible sites of the supernatural in Manatee County, FL. The results were some awesome photographs, And most appreciated, they shared them with this author.

Thanks to author Murray Silver for first inspiring me to look beyond the travel industry for story material, and to all the wonderful people mentioned in my book, who provided needed information and who shared so many experiences with me. I thank each of them for the courtesy extended to me during my period of compiling data. I am unable to name them all in this space, but a special thanks is owed to Robert Edgerly, James Casky, Robert Samuels, Dawn Masters, Jayne James, Marva Almquist, and Lee Pallas, to name just a few.

Dr. Harry Stafford provided a means of my gaining a better understanding of parapsychology, by sharing information on the subject. It was his opinion that I could not possibly do a book dealing with the paranormal without some knowledge of the parapsychology.

To David Nolan, I owe a big "thank you". He came out on Thanksgiving Day to meet with me. He was a huge source of St. Augustine history. He also presented the "other side of the story," by disputing the tales about ghosts and spirits being in the old St. Augustine buildings. To say he is skeptical of the paranormal is putting it mildly, but he certainly provided another interesting side of the subject.

In some instances I have used fictitious names when relating personal experiences, or opinions of those people who would not feel completely at ease with me using their real names. I've tried to respect their wishes in each instance. Their stories, thoughts and beliefs were the ingredients that helped me gather information.

I hope you, the reader, get as much pleasure out of reading "The Shadow Behind You" as I had writing it.

Thanks to all of you! I hope I did you justice. And I would be delighted to hear from any of you who have comments or who want to share your own story with me.

Aline Miller-Musson
k-amusson@prodigy.net

PROLOGUE

The "Shadow Behind You" is something other than a ghost story. It's a look at what is being said about ghosts and other things that go bump in the night. It's also a look at some of the people who tell of seeing or hearing the paranormal beings and it's a look at the findings of some who are said to be experts in their fields.

It's also a book about the extreme hardships faced by the early settlers who looked to this new world as a haven, but who learned it was a place of blood, sweat and tears. A place worth the effort, but a place that took its toll on the hearty pioneers. It follows some of these early settlers from their arrival, to their demise and into what some of the home folk claim is their afterlife, as their spirits drift in and out of the old homes, churches and commercial establishments that still stand in the ancient cities, and preside over their gravesites in mystical fashion.

The tales center on strange things spoken of in some of the cities and towns in the South, especially the cities and towns visited by thousands of vacationers who meander through the streets in Savannah, GA and St. Augustine, FL. It also takes a glimpse at other, more rural Florida and Georgia towns with a peek at the author's own native town, Bradenton, FL. It also lightly sweeps through the hills and valleys of the Appalachians, where a good ghost story is as available as the friendly smile offered there.

There are photographs of some of what the photographers say depicts the phenomena of the supernatural. These are images that usually escape the naked eye, but were captured through the lens of the camera. Orbs and lightening-like streaks, some misty formations and other strange sights said to be paranormal energy, are shared with the readers of this book.

Then there are those who tell of mysterious sights and sounds that fail to produce a clear understanding of what is being seen and heard, but which send a shiver through most of the spines of those experiencing these events.

Some of those with whom we spoke declared the entire paranormal subject is bogus. Someone's vivid imagination. A money-maker for tourist towns. These doubters declare there is not a shred of documentation that prove there is anything unusable happening, or, if something beyond the norm occurs, there is a logical explanation for it that doesn't involve the paranormal.

Visit the cities through the eyes and ears of the author and be amazed by the stories told by folks who live and work there, or agree with the doubters, or join the middle of the road folks on their fence, or just enjoy reading about old places and old stories.

Whether there is something out there prowling around isn't going to be decided by the author. This book is just bringing the information to the readers who may then decide for themselves what they think of "The Shadow Behind You": is it ghost history, or folklore?

IMAGINATION? OR FACT?

Imagine that you are alone at night on a dimly lit street. Imagine that you catch a glimpse of a shadow behind you. You turn to see who is near you and nothing is there.

Imagine that you hear a step behind you. You turn quickly to see who is following you. There's nothing there.

Imagine that you feel a presence, but nothing is visible and there is no place for a person to hide. Nothing is there.

Imagine that there's a strong scent of tobacco smoke that appears to be coming from alongside you. No one near by is smoking. Nothing is there.

Imagine that you feel something brush by you, but nothing is there.

Imagine that you feel a distinct tapping on your shoulder. Thinking a friend has arrived, you turn, but nothing is there.

The temperature is a balmy 75 degrees, as you stroll through the cemetery on a "hunting" expedition with a high tech thermometer in your hand, its beam shooting out several yards from you. Imagine aiming at a distant spot where suddenly the temperature reading on the thermometer drops to 26 degrees. Imagine that the cold spot seems to be moving toward you and finally, seems to stop right in front of you, and lingers for awhile. Is something really there?

These and others, are stories about the supernatural. Truth, or fiction, they hold the attention of most people because they offer the thrill of the unknown. And folks who have experienced these strange events, are strong in their beliefs that there is indeed a world inhabited by the paranormal.

Is this the product of an over-active imagination at work? Or is something very mysterious going on?

Story tellers thrive on this kind of spooky stuff. People hearing the tales react either in total disbelief, or shiver a bit in anticipation of a thrilling story. These, and more, are stories told by people who believe they have had a paranormal experience, have had a friend or family member who has had an encounter with an unknown being, or in some cases, simply do not understand what has happened, but know they have experienced something of the unknown.

While some may embellish somewhat for entertainment purposes, most story tellers recount what they believe they have seen, or what other people have told them they have seen. They share generations of legends handed down throughout the ages.

There probably is not a place on Earth that doesn't shelter people who relentlessly believe in the supernatural. There are thousands of web sites dealing with the paranormal. Books are lined up on the shelves of book stores. Souvenir shops and attractions have items that tell tales about spirits, ghosts and apparitions people have reportedly encountered. Even literature from past ages deals in some form of the supernatural.

Listings of "hot spots," which are tips on where the greatest paranormal activity is, are available at the push of a computer button. There are "how to" instructions from a huge number of national and international organizations that explain how to determine the truth or fallacy of a ghost's existence; how to photograph an apparition; how to record the groans and moans of the ghostly residents; where a person is most likely to find a spirit; how to tell the spirit from the ghost; and how to determine if a building is haunted, just to name a few.

There's a publication, "The Ghost Hunter's Bible" that is advertised as providing the reader everything he or she ever wanted to know about the paranormal. There are photographs being passed around the world portraying what appears to be the mysteries of the supernatural, and there are folks who disprove the authenticity of some of these graphics.

The paranormal plays an integral part in the commerce in areas that are a magnet for tourist traffic. From bustling ancient cities to the lonely mountain roads come tales of the supernatural.

There are millions of stories and untold numbers of story tellers. Always have been. Always will be.

Are these stories about ghost history? Is the story-teller caught up in local folklore and legends, or is he repeating documented facts?

Does the story-teller have an over-active imagination? Or, more simply, is there a logical explanation for the strange events that has nothing at all to do with anything weird or unusual.

Whether the stories are told as the truth, or entertainment, there have always been "believers" and "non-believers" in these tales.

We've dipped shallowly into the surface of a field that is growing in popularity. Numerous people have discussed with us their beliefs in the paranormal. Many of them said not only do they believe in it, they've experienced it. A few adamantly denied the existence of ghosts. Some went so far as to hint that the ghost stories, particularly those around tourist oriented cities, are nothing more than tourist-pleasers that have nothing to do with history, but everything to do with making money.

We've talked to the middle-of-the-road folks who really had no opinion, stating they had never seriously considered the question. Some said they had never seen a ghost, or had a paranormal experience, but do believe something is out there that not everyone can see or hear. Some say that until they experience it, they are not going to believe in the supernatural.

The "ghosts," "spirits," "apparitions," "phantoms" and a multitude of paranormal events we've heard about are mostly about the southern supernatural, not because the South has an exclusivity to the paranormal, but because this is where we wanted to start. This book was inspired by a visit to Savannah, GA, and later ones to St. Augustine, FL, and into the Appalachian Mountains. They've had reputations over the decades for having ghostly beings restlessly prowling the historic byways and out-the-way paths. Some of the specters are sad, some happy, some pleasant and kind and some that are downright mean and ornery, we've been told.

Those in the paranormal "know" tell us there is different terminology for the supernatural. "Apparitions" are manifestations of the soul of a deceased person or animal, but there also are atmospheric apparitions, described as a "visual imprint" of the being that was left behind in the environment from a previous event. There are historical apparitions, which usually are found in older homes and appear in solid forms, recurring apparitions that appear in regular cycles, and many other types of supernatural events.

According to a St. Augustine tour guide a ghost is "residual energy. Spirits, on the other hand, are the paranormal beings who move objects, make noises and reach out to touch people. Other terms we sometimes heard included Phantoms, Shades, and Shadows.

We've strayed from time to time, into states above the Mason-Dixon Line, because folks now living in the South had stories to tell about their experiences in other parts of the country. Since these people are now full-time southerners, we elected to use some of them in our decidedly southern book

Florida and Georgia stack right up there with Louisiana, the Carolinas, Massachusetts and the other 45 contiguous states with having supernatural tales to tell. Even the southern areas not heavily traveled by tourists have mysterious secrets buried deeply within the piney woods, forestlands and final resting places for those pioneers who settled this country and died as a result of their hardships so many decades ago.

. St. Augustine, Florida, and Savannah, Georgia, two of the two-state region's oldest cities have a lot in common. Both are ancient cities. St. Augustine dates back to the 17th and 18th century. Savannah is somewhat newer, with its first documented settlers arriving in the 1700's. Both are sea ports. Both have a proliferation of very old homes and buildings. Both are heavily into the tourist business. And shakers and movers of both cities claim their town is extremely haunted.

Stroll down the streets of the Historic District of Savannah, or St. Augustine's Old City District, browse in the shops, or sit in a restaurant or tavern, and ask anyone you meet if they've experienced, or known anyone who has experienced, a supernatural event. You'll get a surprisingly large number of affirmatives. Folks may have a tale to tell about an eerie sensation, or an unexplained event that they believe could be a haunting experience, or they might tell of a strange event passed on to them by friend or relative that was deciphered as a paranormal happening.

Take a buggy ride, hop on one of the many trolleys or buses, do a walking tour and be regaled with more historical data than you can possibly digest. And along with the factual geographical and ancient history, you will probably hear about the legends, rumors, folklore, and tales about ghosts, tragedies, scandals, and obvious whoppers. Remarkably, every story teller is likely to tell you a different tale about the same event.

Whether the story is about the sequence of ownership of old homes and businesses, the resident ghost that lives there, or any of the myriad facts and figures, the listener is sure to get several different versions from different narrators. Scripts may be the basis for the tour guides, but most ad lib from time to time, and no matter what the facts are, their tales make for interesting and entertaining stories.

Both St. Augustine and Savannah are fertile grounds for haunting stories. Most stories are handed down generation after generation, some come from more recent occurrences, and some may even be manufactured, or embellished upon, to make them a bit more tantalizing.

The nooks and the crannies of the Appalachian Mountains seem to be teeming with paranormal activity and there is an abundance of story tellers to relate the information to anyone willing to listen.

Your author traversed some of the mountains of the Appalachians and listened to the folks who have been hearing about the supernatural for generations. We also took in the sights and tales of both St. Augustine and Savannah and found so many interesting pieces of history and folklore that a book just seemed to be in order. We met some fascinating people and heard some incredible stories. It was a thrilling and interesting ride.

Did we encounter a ghost? No. Not a one. But there were dozens who said they had. Do we believe in the supernatural? This book isn't about this author's belief. It's about the beliefs and the disbeliefs of others and the tales they have to tell. It's a story that has a little bit of history, a little bit of instruction, some tidbits about the tourist attractions and activities, and a lot of mystery.

ST. AUGUSTINE – OLDEST TOWN IN THE NEW WORLD

Enter through the old city gates, that stand as sentries at the northern entrance to St. George Street in St. Augustine, and you have passed through the portals of history.

Although you won't see but a couple of the original buildings of the 16th and 17th centuries, you may feel as if you have just entered the generation of those Spanish warriors that coveted the treasures of Florida. It is through these gates that your experience of entering an ancient city begins.

St. Augustine boasts of being the oldest town in the "new world," having claimed to have played host to Don Juan Ponce de Leon, who led an unsuccessful expedition in an attempt to occupy and settle Florida. He sighted the mainland of the North American continent as he was searching for treasure, and in 1513, named the area La Florida, the "Land of Flowers." But he failed to colonize the north Florida area. Other explorers, including Panfilo de Narvaez,

Hernando de Soto and Tristan de Luna y Arellano, followed Ponce de Leon into the area and all were equally unsuccessful in their endeavor to settle any part of La Florida .

The construction of a fort and colony on the banks of the St. Johns River by the French in 1564 threatened Spain's treasure fleets which sailed along Florida's shores and as a consequence, King Phillip II named Don Pedro Menendez de Aviles governor of Florida in 1565. His tasks were to drive the pirates, or settlers from other countries from the area, and to colonize the territory.

The Castillo de San Marcos was under construction for 23 years, but its endurance can be witnessed today as one of the major tourist attractions in St. Augustine. Constructed mostly of coquina shells, this ancient fort is said to house ghosts of many creeds and nationalities and has even been reported as a site of animal and bird spirits.

It withstood numerous attacks over two hundred years of battle. The English, under the leadership of Sir Francis Drake, burned the town, pirates plundered the area, and greedy explorers sought possession of this new land. English General James Edward Oglethorpe, before settling Savannah, attempted to gain possession of Florida, but failed. And through all the wars, the fort was never overtaken by enemy attack

In 1763 Spain ceded Florida to England, not because of a successful battle, but because it wanted possession of the capital of Cuba. Florida came under English rule in exchange for the Cuban territory.

St. Augustine endured major hardships and disease, all with the background of bloody turmoil, but it always kept its restorative efforts going by returning many colonial structures to their original appearance after they were destroyed by man, nature, or illness.

It was a catastrophic time in the history of the south. In addition to the battles between the new settlers and the Timucuan Indians, the bloody wars over possession of the new land, there were fires, disease and hurricanes with which to contend. As each major catastrophe beset itself upon the territory, the settlers of St. Augustine picked themselves up and fought the battle. Finally, in the early 1800's, Florida became a part of the United States.

A year later, the St. Augustine Historical Society, the oldest continuously operating museum and historical society, formed as an informal group that met in private homes to discuss topics of historical scientific interest.

There had already been destruction of so many historical structures in St. Augustine the need for preservation was strong on the minds of the early colonists.

Two bouts of Yellow Fever, three destructive fires and the hardships of pioneering caused the deaths of thousands of the new citizens. St. Augustine's development was slow and difficult and maintaining the development was even harder.

There are those who credit oil and railroad entrepreneur Henry Flagler, who arrived in St. Augustine in 1885, with the start of progress for the town. But some of residents weren't thrilled over the changes Flagler brought to the quiet pioneer town. And some were downright suspicious of the millionaire who was determined to turn St. Augustine into a destination of the genteel. Some accused him of boastfulness and selfishness. But progress the town did. It gained business after business, as well as impressive structures that today are show places.

The Historical Society continued its endeavor to retain its history. It purchased some of the ancient surviving structures, lost some to the fires, rebounded and purchased others and in 1914 struck a deal with the U. S. War Department to control the fort. In 1935 it became the Castillo de San Marcos National Monument.

Over the years, it was a constant rebuilding operation in St. Augustine. Many of the original buildings that were constructed in the town were wiped out by fires in 1887 and 1914 between the city plaza and the north city gates. Today's St. Augustine, therefore, is a replica of the original, but it harbors the historic relics of a town that struggled to become today's tourist town.

The Shadow Behind You--

Like many old U. S. cities that have suffered from natural disaster, wars and disease, St. Augustine maintains bragging rights for being haunted. Spirits caught up in the death and destruction have reportedly hung around the old town and repeatedly make themselves known to visitors and residents.

SAVANNAH, SHAPED FROM THE WILDERNESS

One of Savannah's 22 squares

    Savannah, Georgia's first city was born in 1733, shaped from wilderness and marshland by Gen. Oglethorpe and his small band of English settlers. The marshland had been home to the Indians and pirates and a few Spanish missionaries prior to its settlement.
    Savannah was established in the early 1700's as a refuge for persecuted Protestants. Gen. Oglethorpe was one of 20 trustees who would administer the colony for its first 20 years.
    Gen. Oglethorpe was instrumental in bringing the threat from the Spanish to an end. After his unsuccessful battle in St. Augustine, he moved on into Georgia, where he sent the Spaniards fleeing from St. Simon Island.
    Gen. Oglethorpe, accompanied by farmers, clothing makers, a baker, carpenters, a druggist and others that lent their talents to the colonizing of the Georgia settlement, was met by the Creek-Choctaw

The Shadow Behind You--

Indians who had already established a small village on the high land of Savannah.

Disease was rampant for those early settlers. More than half of those who arrived in Savannah less than a year before, were dead from Yellow Fever by July, 1733.

A boatload of Jewish explorers from Portugal landed in the settlement and among them was a Jewish physician, Dr. Samuel Nunez, who was welcomed by the open arms of Gen. Oglethorpe, who was trying to cope with the illness and deaths of his people. The Jewish doctor was the first medical person to arrive in this new Georgia land.

Eventually, Gen. Oglethorpe settled the colonists around the squares, where he had the land divided into narrow lots. The "squares" were hardly the masterpieces of beauty they are today. They were sites where battles were fought, hangings were conducted, and the dead were buried. Today they are the centerpiece for the majestic Victorian homes surrounding the squares, and they play a vivid role in tourism in Savannah.

Like their southern neighbors, the early Georgia settlers found a life fraught with hardships, death and destruction.

In addition to the epidemics of Yellow Fever that plagued Savannah, casualties from battle took numerous lives. The second bloodiest battle of the Revolutionary War took place in the heart of Savannah, and during the Civil War it was the prize at the end of the Union army's march through Georgia in 1864. Although much of Georgia was burned by the Union Army, a good portion of Savannah was spared.

At the end of the bloody war, after General William Tecumseh Sherman had led the march to Savannah and won the battle, he gave Savannah to President Abraham Lincoln as a Christmas gift.

Savannah's two dozen squares were the back drop for much of the bloodshed brought about by wars, duels, public executions, and when necessity presented itself, as burial grounds. Today, their beauty and splendor are strewn through the city in the orderly fashion designed by Gen. Oglethorpe. And those who live and visit the stately homes around the squares are convinced that many of the original occupants and those whose lives were lost on the squares, roam the area in ghostly fashion on a regular basis.

Like St. Augustine, Savannah experienced repeated disasters as the scene of major wars, three fires, two bouts of Yellow Fever, turmoil and sorrow. Many of its jewels, the ancient homes and businesses, were destroyed by fire. Only a few 18th century structures remain, and those are located near the waterfront.

Today the historic atmosphere offers the tourist population a haven of 19th century Victorian, Renaissance and other period structures to explore and visit.

Savannah has earned its reputation for weirdness. Its ghosts are said to be plentiful and today's Savannah residents are convinced that their town is indeed among the top most haunted in America.

It, like St. Augustine, was home to the Indians who lived with their many mystics, then was invaded by Pirates such as the famous Blackbeard, and Jean Lafite. Savannah's spirit belongs to sea. Even before the Georgia colony was founded in 1733, the area along the coast from Charleston to St. Augustine, was a dangerous place. Not only was the coastline a battleground for warriors from England and Spain, it also was the habitat for blood thirsty buccaneers who were after the spoils left behind by exploring ships.

Through the ages, the travelers' first experience in Savannah was traversing the cobblestone streets along the riverfront. Today, those cobblestones remain, but the former maritime commerce of the area, has evolved into restaurants, shops and hotels. Cotton mills, warehouses, and other commercial establishments along the waterfront are home to modern day accommodations designed to please the tourist trade.

It is said by some that some of the original residents still "live" in the old buildings.

Like St. Augustine, Savannah is said to be inhabited by countless paranormal beings. Some seem content with their spirit lives, while others prowl the area with restlessness, sadness and anger, legend has it.

EDUCATIONAL PROFILES

It isn't all ghosts and history in the two southern towns.

Both Savannah and St. Augustine also have a high educational profile, which means both cities have a fairly large population of young folks.

Savannah is the home of the Savannah College of Art and Design, a school dedicated to prepare students in the field of arts education. One of the few liberal arts colleges with a degree program in architectural history, the college has been instrumental in restoration projects on old homes in the city. Students there work on restoration projects and receive college credits for their labor.

In the spring of 1979, one year after the Savannah College of Art and Design was legally incorporated in the State, SCAD purchased and renovated the Savannah Volunteer Guard Armory to house the first classroom and administration building. The 1892 building was nominated for inclusion in the National Register of Historic Places. Named Poetter Hall, in honor of Richard G. May, and Paul E. Poetter, founders of the college along with Paula S. Wallace, the building remains an active classroom today.

It offers 69 degree programs with a full university experience in one of the largest and most renowned National Historic Landmark districts in the United States. It offers bachelor of fine arts, master of architecture, master of arts, master of fine arts and master of urban design, along with other course offerings.

Savannah College of Art and Design owns about two million square feet of space in 60 facilities throughout Savannah's historic and Victorian districts.

The Flagler College, a small liberal arts school, is the focal point of St. Augustine's academic atmosphere. Opened in 1968, the school occupies the Ponce de Leon Hall, a former luxury resort hotel now listed on the National Register of Historic Places.

This building of Spanish Renaissance architecture was the dream of Henry Flagler, industrialist, oil magnate and railroad pioneer. Flagler College was established as a memorial to him. More than $43 million has been spent restoring the historic campus and multimillion-dollar auditorium. The campus is in the heart of St. Augustine's old district, sitting on 19 acres of prime property between Cordova and Sevilla Streets. It sits across King Street from Flagler's other former hotel, the Alcazar, which today is the Lightner Museum.

These towns are where southern history was made and where historical events caused the death and suffering of thousands upon thousands. Both are hot beds of superstition. Both cities sit on top of burial grounds as ancient as the towns themselves. Is it any wonder, then, that folks believe both towns are haunted?

THE LOST STATE OF FRANKLIN

Sevier County, TN, like the Georgia and Florida pioneer cities, arose from the ruins of wars and destitution. Claimed by North Carolina's Greene County as part of it's territory when the first settlers arrived, this part of the Appalachian country was known as the State of Franklin.

The entire area had been the hunting grounds for the Cherokee and other eastern tribes of American Indians. Traders from Virginia, however, were attracted to this bountiful area.

Col. Samuel Wear, who fought in the Revolutionary War at the Battle of Kings' Mountain, became a governmental leader of North Carolina, Sevier County and later, the state of Tennessee. Sometime early in 1780, Col. Wear built a fort at the mouth of Walden's Creek, a historical site in Pigeon Forge to this date.

It was 1796 when the State of Franklin movement collapsed and Sevier County and the territory south of the Ohio River ceded to the federal government. Tennessee became a state that same year.

The signing with the Cherokee Nation of the Treaty at Dumplin Creek sometime around 1781 opened the valley surrounded by a beautiful rolling countryside up as fertile land for settlement. Farming, logging and much later, tourism, became the mainstay for the area's economy.

Where today's Eastern Tennessee musical Mecca is located in Pigeon Forge, was a sleepy settlement in the shadows of the Smokey Mountains from the time it was settled in the 1800s until late in the 20th century.

Gatlinburg, noted particularly for its skiing profile, was a bustling tourist town long before folks discovered the tiny Pigeon Forge.

Just as all of the south's settlement, the Smokey's is not without its share of turmoil, wars, fires and disease.

A major accomplishment in the Smokey Mountains was purchase, by the government of more than 500,000 acres of forestland and turning it into a national park.

Through a lot of hard work on the part of an ambitious group of people and the expenditure by Tennessee and North Carolina legislatures of a combined $4 million, the idea of the forest becoming the Great Smoky Mountains National Park seemed to be coming into reality. By 1928, a total of $5 million had been raised through grants, private individuals and groups. Because the fund-raising efforts took so long, the land price had doubled by this time and it was only because of a $5 million donation by the Laura Spellman Rockefeller Memorial Fund that the purchase was completed.

It wasn't until 1940, however, that the transaction was completed. There were dozens of farmers, timber and paper companies that had a stake in land that was becoming government property. It was a heartache for many people, because they were losing not just their land, but the life they had grown accustomed to. Timber cutting, hunting and trapping would no longer be allowed.

And the hills are teeming with legends and folklore and, of course, ghost stories. Every native Appalachian has heard tales that have been handed down from generation to generation. The sadness of many linger on. The hardships of the settlers and those who stuck it out through hard times, left their mark.

The mysteries remain in the hill country as well as the flat land of St. Augustine and Savannah. Some of them are simply mysteries of life and death and others, mysteries of the supernatural.

TAKE A GHOST TOUR AND LET YOUR IMAGINATION RUN FREE

The pages of the south's history books are filled not only with death and destruction, but with superstitions and spiritualism. Indian folklore, English superstitions, Scotch and Irish legends are rampant in Savannah. The Spanish, French and English left their mystic beliefs behind in St. Augustine. Voodoo was an active ancient practice in both the cities.

Like most tourist-oriented cities across the nation, Savannah and St. Augustine are rich in ghost tours. In Pigeon Forge and Gatlinburg, TN, the ghost tour business is getting well heated, as more and more tourists come into the Appalachians with a mind to seek out the paranormal of the hills.

Since the early 1990's, the study of the paranormal has become exceedingly popular and these towns offer the thrills and chills of trudging through the streets of the ancient cities by the light of the moon, listening to a talented narrator tell tales about ghostly beings drifting through old homes, cemeteries, businesses, and historical monuments. Ghosts are big business in tourist towns. People are eager to hear a scary story and leave the gate open for a possible personal encounter with a ghostly being.

Even the scoffers are given food for thought when they accompany a tour of would-be ghost hunters, and though they don't admit to the expectation of experiencing any kind of paranormal event, they are along for the ride anyhow, and are among the first in any ghost tour to heft their digital cameras toward the darkness in hopes of capturing the supernatural in their lens.

As ghost tours go, one of the more educational tours may be the one operated by Dr. Harry Stafford. "Paranormal Investigative Tours in St. Augustine," gives tour groups a crash course on finding and studying the paranormal. Dr. Stafford has studied extensively, the subject of parapsychology. He has also been involved in ghost hunting expeditions and is heavily involved with the study of all things phenomenology, causes and consequences of paranormal experiences.

Parapsychology is defined by the Psychology Foundation as the study of "apparent anomalies of behavior and experience that exist apart from currently known explanatory mechanisms. The foundation claims that modern-day parapsychology could be regarded as "a kind of off-shoot or extension from psychology." It also sees a need for a continued cooperative effort on the part of psychologists and parapsychologists to learn as much as possible about the paranormal.

Dr. Stafford said Parapsychology involves not only field work dealing with the scientific investigation of alleged hauntings, but also includes laboratory work focusing on controlled, laboratory studies of mind-matter interactions, distant healing, clairvoyance, precognition and other studies in consciousness.

Dr Stafford's tours begin with an orientation and instruction period, which familiarizes participants with the use of an electromagnetic field meter, issued for the walk. The tour participants are given an opportunity to experience an interactive walking tour which introduces them to the investigation of haunted sites. Dr. Stafford or his trained field personnel, give lessons on how to assess the genuine haunting of a site.

Teacher and author, Dr. Stafford has dealt in the paranormal for a number of years.

Tour personnel share stories of events from previous tours, and give participants historical facts about the areas they are visiting. At the end of the tour there's a time for discussion about what the participants have witnessed, and a time to look through the photos to see what tours past have witnessed.

Participants are encouraged to share photos they have taken while on Dr. Stafford's tours. They also are invited to browse through the album of photos from previous tours. Sightings not visible to the naked eye often show up in the photos, he said. However, he added, participants have experienced an occasional sighting, paranormal sounds, scents and tactile encounters.

He cautioned that not everything that shows up in the photograph is paranormal. Sometimes the environment interferes with the photo-taking and objects that are interpreted as orbs and other phenomena are just drops of moisture.

"This is a learning experience, but we hope people also enjoy themselves," Dr. Stafford said.

The St. Augustine nightly ghost hunters start off at the corner of Cuna and Charlotte, just off the St. George historic area. They view the mysteries of the central old district area, homes and buildings said to harbor ghostly beings. Across from the Old City gates, the 20-some ghost seekers trek through Castillo de San Marcos, the old fort and courtyard, with digital cameras whirring. If the photographer is lucky, he or she may walk away with a photo that has an object in it that wasn't seen in the camera lens by the naked eye. If there aren't any spirits stirring in the old fort this night, the crowd is given hope that another site may yield some sightings. The group will be led through the historical streets of St. Augustine, taking in the mystery of a couple of old cemeteries, where orbs and misty forms have often been portrayed in the camera lens, the eeriness of ancient buildings. Throughout the 90 minutes of the tour, guides will lend their knowledge of the supernatural for both the believers and the non-believers.

Tours are common in tourist towns. Places like Savannah, Atlanta, Key West, FL, St. Augustine, Orlando, and other southern cities such as those in North and South Carolina, and Tennessee have a wide menu of tours, but for the most part in all areas, the night time emphasis is decidedly on ghost tours. Ghost hunting expeditions have become big business in this country, and especially in the tourist-oriented towns across.

In St. Augustine, the first tours consisted of two guides who felt lucky to take a combined dozen people through the streets in a night. The popularity quickly grew. First, a couple dozen certified guides were required, then to the hundreds of tour guides busily showing the travelers the darkest corners of the city every night of the week.

Savannah, Georgia's oldest city, is a "walking tour of three centuries of history," says author Murray Silver.

Silver, who was launching his latest book, "Behind the Moss Curtain," when we ran into him along the Savannah waterfront, insisted that no article can ever be written about Savannah without exploring the subjects of ghosts and bed and breakfasts facilities.

"These are the two hottest commodities here," he said.

Savannah offers its visitors a myriad of nighttime thrillingly scary attractions, with a multitude of tours crawling through the streets and pubs. There are stops in front of old homes and old businesses, and a walk through the cemeteries, or as close to them as city ordinance permits. The tours traverse Savannah's many historical squares, where death and mayhem were reportedly common. Savannah, the scene of wars, destructive fires, disease, hangings and other gruesome activities, is fodder for the ghost seeker.

Among the many tourist contributions in Savannah is the nightly "Hauntings Tour," a 90-minute walking tour operated by Robert Edgerly. Billed as a saunter in Savannah, the "Hauntings Tour" takes in a variety of places teeming with history.

He conducts daytime tours, Savannah Saunter, that explore the amazing architectural offerings, the lovely southern gardens and historical landmarks of historical Savannah. He also conducts a "Homemade Thunder" tour which delves into the Civil War. "The Pirate's Walk, which features true tales of treasure and sea rovers of the past, is another of his offerings. His tour company, dealing in both the mystical and the realistic history of Savannah, makes its headquarters at the corner of Bull and York Streets. The nightly ghost tours negotiate near-by Wrights Square, site of many 18th and 19th Century hangings, then treks through the city's historical district to favorite haunting places.

Edgerly says much of Savannah's haunted history is intertwined with recorded incidents, which he says tends to give credence to the many ghost stories woven into the 90-minute walk.

He has recently expanded into the mountains of Tennessee, with "Smokey Mountains Tours" offering nightly ghost expeditions in

The Shadow Behind You--

the Gatlinburg and Pigeon Forge areas. Edgerly's relatively new operation joins a proliferation of tours already searching for the unknown in the mountainous regions of Pigeon Forge, Gatlinburg, and Ashville, offered by "Haunted Ghost Tours." His "Hauntings Tours" meet at the "Needle" in downtown Gatlinburg and traverse the back ways and out-of-the-way places that the average tourist might not see were it not for this walking adventure. It takes in some creepier areas of the Smokeys in its search for the hill country spirits of yesteryear.

"There are sights in those mountains that can make chill bumps pop out Edgerly predicts. He says his participants get the opportunity to walk through streets of Gatlinburg that is not seen by the hurrying crowds gathering around the commercial area.

Edgerly is an absolute believer. The Savannah native has been a history buff for years and has explored many aspects of the settlement, growth, destruction and re-growth of Savannah. His Georgia heritage spans many years, and he said he has grown up with stories about the paranormal.

"Do I believe in the paranormal? You bet I do," Edgerly asserts.

James Caskey operates the "Savannah Haunted History Tour," and the "Savannah Spirts Haunted Pub Crawl. His pub crawl offers "both types of spirits," and not unexpectedly, the pub crawl is extremely popular.

"It explores two of Savannah's time-honored traditions: ghosts and alcohol," he says of his Pub Crawl.

It took some personal experiences with the supernatural to make Caskey a believer. He said he arrived in Savannah from Florida without a single idea there was such a thing as ghosts. But it didn't take long for his views to change drastically, as we will detail later in this book.

The ancient River Street has its share of frightening tales to be told as well. "Pirate's Walk" tour-goers carefully navigate the aged cobblestone streets of River Street, and listen to "blood curdling tales of swashbucklers, buccaneers and sea-rovers of yesterday."

The Shadow Behind You--

Occasionally, an unearthly figure is reported in the old merchant's area along the river. A particular tale is one told by many tour guides of the chilling atmosphere in the liquor room in a restaurant on River Street. The owner doesn't like visiting the room and the staff members refuse to enter it. Inside a former warehouse, the room is said to be haunted by a slave who died there.

Also among ghostly offerings in Savannah is the "Ghost Talk Ghost Walk," which bills itself as the original ghost talk walk that takes a "fun and enlightening approach to the legends that lie beneath the haunting tales of Savannah."

"Ghosts & Gravestones," is a far-reaching tour operation. Operated by "Old Town Trolley Tours." It has tours in Boston, Washington DC, San Diego, Key West and St. Augustine, as well as Savannah. A riding tour on the "Trolley of the Doomed," where tales of murder, ghosts and other mysterious phenomena are shared by the "Gravedigger" guides decked out in funereal attire to add to the atmosphere, the nightly events across the nation promise to explore the most haunted places in the town.

It promises Savannah "Ghosts & Gravestones" sightseers a glimpse of the house that underwent an exorcism. This is the Hampton Lillibridge House on East St. Julian Street, where an Episcopal bishop spent 45 minutes in a ceremony to cleanse the house of evil spirits. The exorcism was in 1963, after the house had reportedly been haunted by evil spirits for some years. Restoration work on the house, which had been moved from another location, went exceedingly slow because workers were constantly confronted with frightening events. Sounds of a jazz band that wafted through the air at times, put a rakish slant on the experiences, leading folks to believe some of the spirits were enjoying themselves.

In St. Augustine, the "Ghosts and Gravestones" tour takes Florida visitors to what it terms as the "three most haunted sites in St. Augustine." The Old Drug Store, built on an Indian burial ground; the Spanish Military Hospital, the site of many ghost trackers' investigations; and the Old Jail, which housed the city's criminals in days gone by, are included in the lineup of frightening places to go.

The Shadow Behind You--

The frightful attraction bills itself in St. Augustine as the "city's premier 'Frightseeing tours".

Not to be outdone by Savannah in the "spirits" commodity, St. Augustine also boasts of its Haunted Pub Tour, which takes the visitor on a storytelling excursion through "bewitching" destinations. Highlight of the tour are the stops at several local pubs which are home to "ghosts that just won't go away."

Easily matching Savannah in ghostly offerings, St, Augustine also can boast of having Ripley's Believe It or Not Museum as a part of its assets. The museum, which features the haunted castle, has added its own spooky tour to its offerings. "Mysteries of the Castle Warden Hotel," is being offered by the original Ripley's Believe It or Not museum.

History tells us that in 1944, a mysterious fire killed two women at the Castle Warden Hotel home of the museum. Although there have been reports of ghostly beings in and around the museum, this particular tour emphasizes giving participants clues to solving the mysteries surrounding the tragedy.

The Ripley's organization owns a huge plot of Gatlinburg's two-mile downtown entertainment district. Not only does it have the Ripley's Believe it or Not Museum, but it also owns Ripley's Aquarium of the Smokeys, Ripley's 4D Theatre, and Ripley's Haunted Experience.

The original ghost tour in St. Augustine was started in 1994 by Sandy Craig and Karen Harvey. Craig, whose St. Augustine heritage goes back 400 years, owns the "Tour St. Augustine." She began offering non-ghostly tours to school groups on overnight field trips. She wanted the students to enjoy themselves and at the same time, learn something about the history of St. Augustine. And history of St. Augustine is compelled to included stories about ghosts and spirits.

"All of our stories are researched through records from historical writings," Craig said. These include such things as personal diaries, Church papers and historical library documents.

"Nothing is made up and no artificial special effects are used during the tour. Everything you see is real," she says.

The first tours were operated with two guides. A mere handful of would-be ghost hunters expressed an interest in the first tours. Soon, though, the tour founders said, the popularity grew for the expeditions. More than 20 professional storytellers are now a part of the tour, that stroll through the streets, ride in trolleys, or sit back and enjoy the sea breeze on boat tours. Nightly there are a variety of ghost tours to be taken.

Lee Pallas, who joined Craig and Harvey early in the ghost tour's inception, said the tour is based on "legends of ghosts and other strange experiences in St. Augustine."

"Tour St. Augustine" also has on-and-off tours, walking tours, educational tours and other special tours, and covers a wide spectrum of historical facts.

Craig's tour operations include, in addition to the trolley tour, "Ghostly Express," a boat tour, "Ghosts of the Matanzas," which is a theatrical cruise along the Matanzas Bay.

Pallas half jestingly promises occasional bloody tours down the bay when it manifests itself into a river of "blood of all those who lost their lives in the waters." He swears the waters turn red every now and again. And that may be an example of the tall tales that are a part of the ghostly repertoire.

The tour business also offers an hour-long walking ghost tour, led by tour guides that include Matt McCarthy, who wields an old fashion lantern as he treks through St. Augustine's monuments and historical sites. Altogether, "Tour St. Augustine" employs about 25 tour guides.

Folks taking ghost tours in St. Augustine have reported having encountered see an image of an American Indian at the old fort, and some people claim to have seen ghostly animals and fowl. A favorite story among some tour story tellers is the lady in the Ancient City who silently washes her clothes. She looks neither to the left nor the right. Just continues washing them, as tour groups pass by, McCarthy says.

The Shadow Behind You--

Along with the many older tours in the old city are new ones that are born daily, it seems.

Dawn Masters owns a more recently established tour, the "St. Augustine Spirit Stroll Ghost Tour." She also works with Dr. Stafford, and has done some paranormal investigation. Her nightly candle-lit strolls are designed to help visitors discover the history, mystery and hauntings of the old city, Masters declares.

Other groups such as the three different tours offered by "Ghost Tours of St. Augustine," "Ghosts and Hauntings," and a tour, "The Original Sheriff's Ghost Walk," that is advertised to be a "ghostly adventure" conducted by an early 1900's sheriff or his "deputies," as well as the "Ghosts and Gravestones," tours are just a smattering of the numerous supernatural offerings to the St. Augustine visitor.

These are only the "haunted" tours. There are dozens that deal with history and throw in some legend and folklore with the history lesson. Others are just offered to the tourist to enjoy the view, but these too offer the participant some "facts" and sometimes "fiction" about the town they are visiting.

An interesting new and unique tour operation has started in St. Augustine. The Convention Bike Tour is one that veers slightly off the ghostly path and offers a "fun" trip for six folks who like to pedal bicycles.

David Saunders expects to have a huge success with the Convention Bike Tour. This novel new vehicle is a contraption with an octagon-shaped frame supporting seven sets of pedals, and seven seats. One of the seats and set of pedals will always be occupied by the lead tour guide who steers the bicycle.

"It's a very interesting concept," Saunders said.

Eric Staller, inventor of the Conference Bike, did a demonstration for the students of the Florida School for the Deaf and Blind, which is headquartered in St. Augustine. Students took turns on the unusual bike.

"They really loved it," Saunders said.

The Shadow Behind You--

Both Savannah and St. Augustine share their streets and roadways with horse and buggy rides, walking history tours, bike tours, scooter tours, trolley history tours, buggy tours, scenic boat cruises and a host of other tourist attractions, all dealing in the history, beauty and the mysteries of the old cities.

A tour operator who previously made regular runs between Kissimmee and St. Augustine, has recently opened a new operation that takes tourists from the Kissimmee area to over-night tours in places like Atlanta and Macon, GA; Charlotte S. C., and Savannah, Nashville and Memphis, TN and St. Louis.

Marva Almquist, who operates "Marvelous Adventures, Inc." had some trouble getting all the official red tape tied together to launch the tours which combine bus transit, scenic and historical lodging, meals and entertainment. The new series of tours, "Adventures in Southern Hospitality," join her other varied offerings dealing in the travel and tourist industry.

Two of her tours involve the Savannah area. Luxury tour buses regularly depart the St. Cloud, FL area and surrounding cities on monthly tours to the historic area. The road portions of the trips are enlivened by professional actors who will play the parts of fine 1800's southern ladies. They regale the tour-goers with stories, comedy, song and dance.

Once they reach Savannah, they will be housed in the Historic District and treated to fine southern cooking in such famous restaurants as The Lady and Three Sons, the scene of daily block-long lines of diners at lunch and dinner time. Included in the tour fare will be several activities, including a ghost tour and a dinner-boat adventure, buggy rides where narrators will share historical facts, and other tourist attractions.

The Nashville tour offers a stay in the Opryland Hotel, and of course, since it's Nashville, after all, tour participants will also be treated to a show at the Grand Ole Opry.

In St. Louis, travelers get the opportunity to be a part of the Riverboat Race of the Belle of Louisville," while Memphis will feature the gyrations of "Elvis," among other fun activities.

The "Ghost Experience" previously operated by "Marvelous Adventures," between the Orlando-Kissimmee area and St. Augustine, has been halted, except for special group excursions. The bus trip had taken folks to St. George Street in St. Augustine, and started its "Ghost Experience" at about 8 p.m. They took in the Hugenot Cemetery, the Old Jail, where they were treated to a view of the glow where the "ghost of Sheriff Jackson still hangs out." The two-and-a half hour trip to St. Augustine included dinner.

"The problem was the late hour we returned to the Kissimmee area," Almquist said.

"Most of my patrons were rather elderly and they didn't like the long drive home. They didn't get back to the area until midnight or after," she said.

A busy lady, she is dominant in the Central Florida travel industry.

These are far from the total tour offerings in the south. They are but a sampling of what goes on daily from sunup until near the bewitching hour in historic towns all over America. They are the tours that are noticed, but there are quiet little groups that go hunting for the paranormal in non-tourist towns, as well. But for this book, we will concentrate on the tourist tours.

TOUR GROUPS NOT UNIVERSALLY LOVED

The tourists love the tours. The Tourist Associations know the tours add to the business activity in tourist towns, and most businesses in these towns recognize the advantages of having tour groups trailing through the historic districts.

But not everyone loves the groups who trail through the streets after dark. Nor does everyone love the stench of the horses drawing the carriages full of tourists, especially at the end of a long hot day. And the traffic jams created by slow-moving vehicles stopping at area sights to give their passengers a lesson in history of the area sometimes cause tempers to rise.

It particularly hasn't been all smooth sailing for the ghost tours.

Craig and her partner faced opposition immediately upon launching their ghost expeditions in St. Augustine, according to Lee Pallas.

Pallas remembered that there was some resistance from the town's people, when she first added the ghostly adventures to her tour business.

"Since this is a Victorian city, such activities as ghost tours were often frowned upon," said Pallas.

But the merging of the history of St. Augustine and of legends, folklore and historical sightings of paranormals in a tour was a natural and soon was in huge demand. Since its popularity has been growing since its inception, it was not a business that city fathers could afford to turn their backs upon. It was a tourist attraction in a tourist town, and those involved in the tourist industry were happy to see some additional activity.

But still there are complaints. Some people just simply don't want groups lolling around in front of their homes or places of business. Some don't like the idea of groups sprawling off the sidewalks and sometimes in the streets in the historic areas. Today, it would seem that St. Augustine residents and business people are more concerned with the nuisance value of the tours than they are with the Victorian attitudes.

The Shadow Behind You--

The St. Augustine City Commission has dealt with some of the complaints. Its director of Public Affairs held meetings with tour owners in an effort to work out a plan that would satisfy the disgruntled merchants and residents

An agreement was reached that called for the groups going to areas other than residential when they are requested not to bring them there, and to bypass businesses that complained about tours stopping in front of their premises.

Stafford, who participated in the joint effort, said most business, especially those dealing with the hospitality industry, welcome the groups that visit them. However, he added, there "have been some complaints."

An inn in the heart of the Old Town District was particularly disturbed by groups lingering in front of the establishment, he said.

"So we avoid that corner now," he added.

There were complaints reported by residents near the Lighthouse Park, who said tour groups were going onto the small dock which was reportedly the scene of a 19th century tragedy. This dock, one of the commissioners reported, was too small for large groups, and was used for pleasure by the residents of the neighborhood. These residents weren't thrilled with having 20 or so people crowding onto the dock to get a glimpse of the site of the drowning of three small children in the 1800's. The narrowness of the streets leading through the residential area to the old lighthouse also added to the problems, the residents said.

But the Lighthouse tour has been sanctioned by the Lighthouse Museum, the city officials said, and has been expanded to allow tour participants to climb the 219 steps the top of the reportedly haunted tower. Nevertheless, tour participants aren't encouraged to explore the dock anymore.

"Some are a bit touchy about that," Pallas, whose tour goes to the area regularly, admitted.

Records indicate there are more than 300 licensed tour guides in St. Augustine, and for the most part, the guides respect the wishes of residents.

"Tour guides are careful to abide by the city's wishes," Pallas said. "None of them want to be a nuisance."

Some of the residents do not want a group of 20 or more people standing in front of their house waiting for the appearance of a ghost," Pallas said.

A NEW "BELIEVER" IN ST. AUGUSTINE

David Saunders, the new tour entrepreneur, is a relatively newly recruited believer in the paranormal. He may well be one of the most enthusiastic we spoke to on the St. Augustine paranormal scene. He's had a couple of experiences and he literally gets chill bumps when he talks about them.

Formerly he scoffed at the idea of the paranormal, but today he is a changed individual.

He was a staffer for the Old St. Augustine Village, a branch facility of the Museum of Arts & Sciences in Daytona Beach. Visitors to this facility are given guided tours of the nine historical houses spanning the period 1790 to 1910. Visitors may also amble at will through the grounds and most of the houses. The Old Village is one of the many historical attractions in the city, but is said to be the site of an early 16th century settlement.

The site, bounded by St. George, Bridge, Cordova and Palm Row, was included in the 1572 town plan. Archeological evidence points to early structures such as a 16th century church, a cemetery, a hospital, and other early edifices.

In later years, the land became a community of nine 18th and 19th century homes. The oldest, The Murat House, was built in late 1700's. A progression of owners of the home that is said to have hosted the nephew of Napoleon Bonaparte, changed its appearance and in 1941, Kenneth Dow purchased the house, then quickly acquired the other eight houses that now make up the Old Village.

There's a lot of history in the Old Village, but for purposes of this book, the real story about the village began in 2004, when Saunders joined the staff there.

A former art director and photographer, Saunders is a photographer who enjoys doing landscapes, wild life and captures some of the local architectural beauty in his lens from time to time.

The Shadow Behind You--

Hired as a groundskeeper and a part-time host to the Old Village visitors, Saunders lived onsite for a period, in an upstairs apartment of the Dow House.

But during Saunders' stay there, he encountered some of the spirit energy said to be living in the old houses, he says. And he has photos to prove it. Even after moving down the street from the "Old Village," he managed to take a startling photo which he says depicted the essence of a woman who resembles a previous resident, Ms. Sarah McKinnon.

Saunders tells this story about his encounter with what he thinks is the apparition of Ms. McKinnon.

In February, 2006, a young couple that was honeymooning in St. Augustine stopped for a visit to the Old Village. It was near the end of the day and Saunders was working at the General Store, where tickets are sold to tour the houses.

About a half hour after the young couple purchased their tickets, they appeared back at the store. The lady said she had felt a "presence" in the Dow House.

The couple, as they approached the house, had walked up to the door near the kitchen and knocked on it. They were relatively sure the house was empty, since they were two of the last people touring the attraction, so their knock was described as "a kind of joke."

Imagine their surprise when a return knock sounded from above.

They repeated the knock and the sound from above came again. Thinking perhaps someone actually was upstairs, they entered the house cautiously, but not in fright.

Immediately upon entrance, both sensed a "weird" feeling. They got goose bumps and had a tingling in their bodies, Saunders said they told him.

Frightened, they left the house and returned to the store to tell about their experience. They thought the sounds were coming from the attic of the house. They declined the invitation to return to the house with Saunders. In fact, they decided their time at the village had expired.

Although Saunders had photographed some paranormal energy in his former home, he had never encountered a supernatural being. He said he had stored some of his belongings in the attic while he lived there, and had never felt fright or had any hesitation about entering it "even alone and after hours."

He turned his duties over to another staff member, grabbed his camera and headed to the house. In the one attic, he just "aimed and shot in different corners of the room, using auto focus mode on my camera." Without looking at the images on his digital camera, he went to the other attic and repeated his actions.

"And that's where I captured the ghostly image of Sarah McKinnon," he said, although at the time, he said he didn't know he was capturing anything and had not even been that acquainted with the photos on the premises of Ms. McKinnon.

When he went back to the office, he reviewed the frames. All the other images showed nothing that he hadn't seen with his naked eye. One, though, "scared the daylights out of me."

The photo of the misty formation shows what could be a face, with a prominent view of what appears to be a human nose. And, according to Saunders, the nose is "identical" to the nose of Ms McKinnon. He thought it looked familiar, and one of the staffers thought it looked a little bit like a lady depicted in the video that is shown to visitors as they begin their tour. Saunders reviewed the video and is now convinced the face in his photograph could be that of Ms. McKinnon, one of the long-time residents of the historical home.

Saunders believes she was not pleased with folks prowling around her attic home when she made her presence known.

"She frightened me," Saunders said. "Every time I enter the house now, I get goose bumps. I'm going to start calling them ghost bumps," he laughingly added.

Saunders emphasizes that his pictures which seem to show paranormal energy are just as he shot them.

The Shadow Behind You--

"They are not retouched in any way. I shot them and my professional processor developed them," he insists.

What came from that lens sent shivers through his spine.

Historical records report that prior to the purchase of the Dow house by Kenneth Dow in 1941, he and longtime resident Sarah McKinnon agreed that she would have a lifetime tenancy in the "Yellow" House on bridge Street. She lived to be 103 and continued her residency there until her death.

"I think she is living here, now. I think she's in the Dow House attic," Saunders said. Furthermore, he added, "I don't think she wants to be bothered.

The Dow House in the Old Village of St. Augustine. Is it still the home of Sarah McKinnon? Does her spirit live on in the old yellow house?

The Shadow Behind You--

Above, Sarah McKinnon, as she appeared in this early photo. Look closely nest to the arrow in the photo below and find the tip of what appears to be a nose which Saunders believes is identical to Ms. McKinnon's.

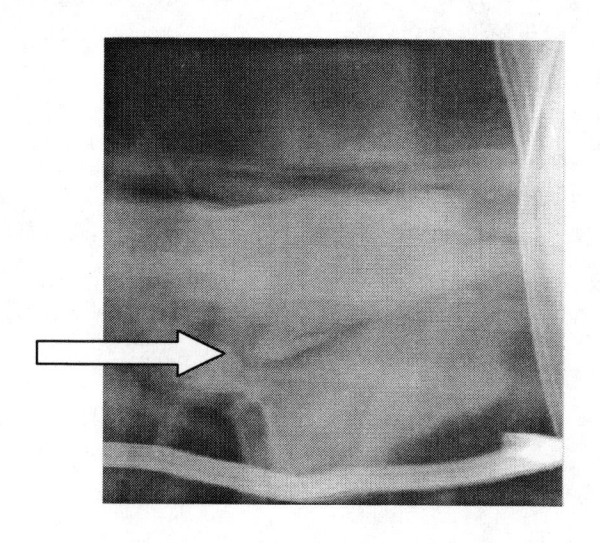

The Shadow Behind You--

The Dow house, originally constructed by the Canova family, was owned by Mary Hayden, the widow of a prosperous hotel owner. In 1905, she had had the frame Territorial Period house moved from its original site on St. George Street, a short distance to the Old Village.

After Kenneth Dow bought the house in 1941, he engineered a series of expansions and repairs on the old home. A year before, he had purchased the house next door, called the Prince Murat House. Ten years later, he had purchased all nine of the historic houses within this block and in 1989; he donated the property, houses filled with fine art, antiques and family heirlooms to the museum.

With all that history, it probably should not have come as a surprise to Saunders when unexplainable events began occurring.

"Nothing paranormal had ever occurred to me before I came here. I was not a believer," Saunders said. But now, he has several encounters to tell about.

His first encounter was not even recognized as an encounter when it happened, he said, while first being interviewed for this book.

It was a nice spring evening, just after dark and he was sitting outside gazing toward the Prince Murat House. He noticed a light on in the second floor bathroom of the house. The attraction was closed for the day and besides, he explained, the old bathroom in the Murat house was never open to the public.

"So there was no reason for the light to be on," he said.

He admits he didn't go check on the light. In fact, he said he was a bit nervous, because "I actually wondered if we had a trespasser on the property." The duties of "groundkeeper," he admitted with a grin, did not include hunting down trespassers, and besides, he figured there was a logical reason behind the light in the bathroom, and dismissed it from his mind.

It bothered him enough, though, to make him seek out the person who closed the facility the night before, and ask why the light was left on.

The staff member swore the light wasn't on when he left the premises. A look at the house and its many rooms assured the staff there was no trespasser on the property at this time. At least there did not appear to be a trespasser that was visible to the naked eye. The light also was not on when the staff did its investigation.

"I didn't know what to think," Saunders said. "I knew I had seen a light shining in that window."

He kept a wary eye turned toward the Murat house over the next few nights, and sure enough, come dark and he could see that the light was on. For several evenings, the light shined out the window and Saunders became more and more suspicious that something was going on next door. Then, as suddenly as it had appeared, it stopped appearing.

Saunders said he had no answer for the phenomena, but he started hearing tales about the village being haunted. And it got his interest into high gear. Still not completely a "believer," he was at least exploring the possibility that the light was turned on and off by something that was not part of the normal scheme of things.

A visitor to the village told the staff that she was certain there was a spirit in the Murat House One of the oldest surviving Colonial structures in St. Augustine; the 1790 house was a boarding house when it was owned by the Canova family in the 1800's. Prince Achille Murat, nephew of Napolean Bonaparte, is reported to have boarded at the house at one time.

Several reports have been made from many people about the ghost of what appeared to be a Spanish soldier who seemed to be guarding various structures in the area of the Dow and Murat houses. There were reports of repeated visits by the soldier to a rented apartment on Hypolita Street and at the Pellicer-Peso de Burgo house on St. George Street, all within a few blocks of the Dow and Murat homes.

"Maybe it was the Spanish soldier who left the light on," Saunders mused.

Leah Green, who was touring the Old Village structures rushed into the General Store one day, exclaiming she had felt the presence of spirits in the village and particularly in the store, which also houses the admission office.

"They're happy spirits, though," she assured the staff. She said she especially felt joy in the presence in the General Store.

"Which made sense to me, because this General Store building once housed a kindergarten and later, a doll and toy store and a millinery shop before being transformed into two apartments for women of the deMedicis family in 1921," said Saunders.

The deMedicis family, prominent business owners in the late 1800's, had also owned and occupied the Canova House just east of the store building.

"There must have been a lot joy in that area, so naturally, there should be happy ghosts there," Saunders guessed.

More and more, Saunders was getting "hooked" on the belief that some spiritual beings definitely occupied many of the old houses in which he worked by day, and which were his neighbors by night, for a period.

"One of my hobbies is photography and I use a conventional camera to take my photos," Saunders said.

"I was advised to get a throw-away camera and take some random photos at night, just to see what I might see in the finished product. And I did," he noted.

He took various photos – some specific and some random shots of his ceiling and other areas of his apartment, then took the camera to his favorite processing center for development. When he received the prints, he noticed five had not been developed and a look at the contact sheet told why. It was the shop's practice not to develop frames that were blurred and the contact sheet showed some extremely blurred frames. In a couple of the photos, there were objects that were totally unexplainable.

He returned to the shop and asked that prints be made of the five missing frames and what he got was a shock not only to him, but to the film processor as well. Streaking across his ceiling was a series of squiggles, columns, and jags, and in at least one, the faint image of what could be a transparent man running away. Another pictures a friend standing before a door and the photo shows two distinct white bars stretching across the front of the lady.

"The guy who does my developing said he had never seen anything like this and certainly, neither had I," exclaimed Saunders.

All of the objects in the photos were diagnosed by those who claim to know, as energy – as in paranormal energy.

"I became a believer immediately," he said, then added, "look at me, I'm getting goose pimples just telling you about it."

"One of his friends, Dawn Masters, owned a "ghost finder." The electromagnetic field finders are available in shops in St. Augustine, Saunders said. Saunders said he hadn't seen the equipment in operation, so following a group meeting in his apartment which dealt with the paranormal, his friend and he were relaxing. She had brought the ghost finder with her, so she demonstrated it for Saunders.

"It was amazing," Saunders recalled.

Masters said she had known Kenneth Dow, who had died three years previously. She thought quite highly of him. She also knew some of the family history, so she asked Kenneth if he was present. Immediately she got a response from the machine.

She started asking questions of Kenneth.

"That meter went wild," he recalled. "I'm going to get one."

Jayne James, another friend, was also a guest of Saunders that evening. She said she too owns an electromagnetic field finder, but she did not have it with her that evening.

"When I got home, my machine was just going wild," she recalled.

A few nights later, James, took her machine to the Murat house and "I talked to the Dows there," she said.

Although it was something of a shock to Saunders to realize that he might be living in a haunted apartment, he said he was never uncomfortable while living there.

"I didn't feel threatened, at all," he said. Before his latest encounter, he declared that the spirits in the Old Village "seem to be friendly ghosts."

Previously, a paranormal research team investigated Old St. Augustine Village. The team reportedly picked up numerous presences in their electro-magnetic meters. Some photographs of orbs were captured as well.

Adding to the fact the village appears to be one of the ghost "hot spots," is the superstition it harbors as well. One of its prestigious live residents was Missy Dean, St. Augustine's "Voodoo queen."

Missy Dean, who reportedly practiced Voodoo with chickens, lived in the Spear House, an 1899 one-story structure with a tower, which today is the museum at the village. Dow, who was acquainted with Missy Dean, described her as a "colorful eccentric."

Night-time tour guides sometime accuse Missy Dean of tampering with cameras which might get near the top of the old wall surrounding the village.

The Old St. Augustine Village is an integral part of St. Augustine's history and it has seen its share of heartache, so anything is possible.

The Murat House. Another haunted house in the Old Village?

The Shadow Behind You--

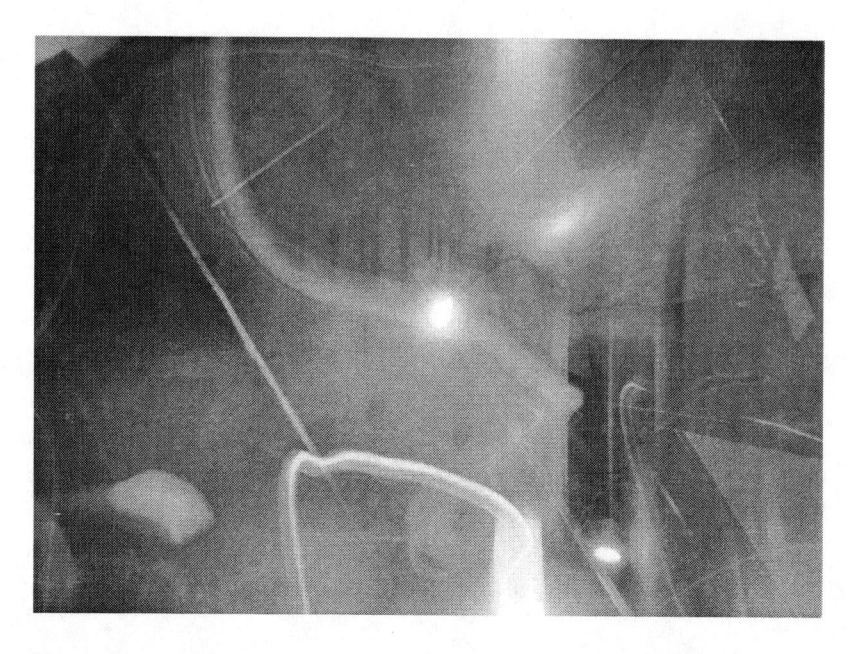

Photo was taken in an ordinary apartment. Furnishings are hidden by the unusual objects that showed up in the developed film

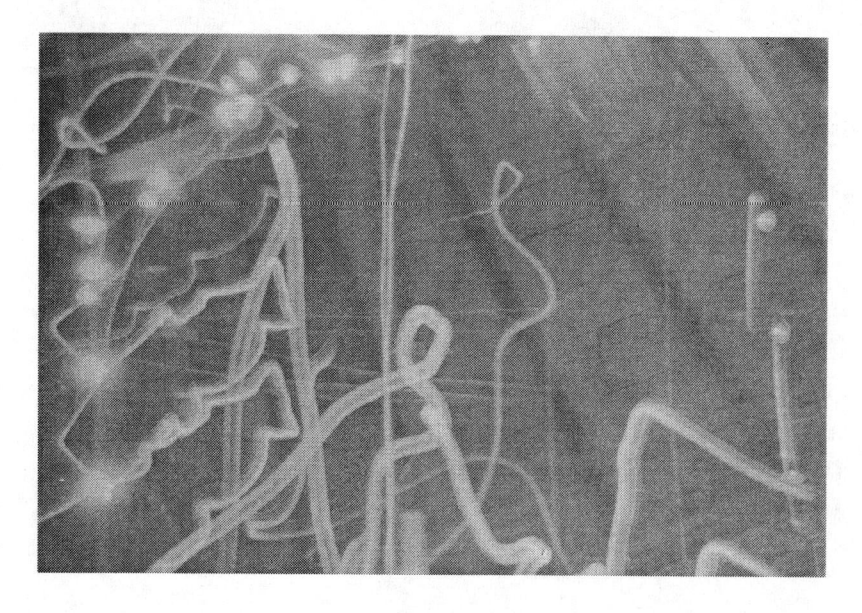

The Shadow Behind You--

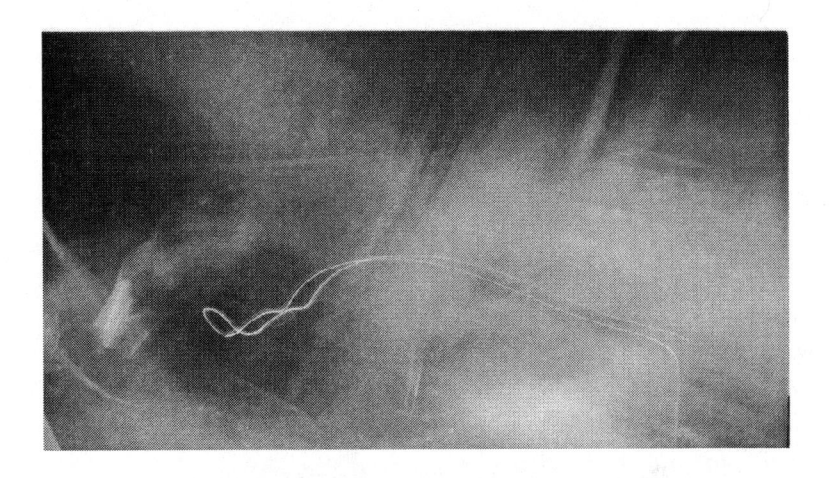

More squiggles in the Old Village house

Figure pictured in bottom photograph is a real person. The streak Of light in front of her was not viewable by the naked eye.

CEMETERIES - FERTILE GROUND FOR GHOST STORIES

Cemeteries, the final resting place for the dead, have always been fertile ground for scary stories. Youngsters through the ages have delighted in pulling pranks on other youngsters in cemeteries. History buffs scour cemeteries hunting for ancient gravestones, hoping for a glimpse into the past, or perhaps location of some lost ancestor. Some folks are frightened of cemeteries at night, while others are anxious to learn what is stirring around the old gravestones. The very nature of an old cemetery makes it a prime location for all of the ghost tours in any town.

There are those who claim old cemeteries could be locations for access ports into the next dimension for spirits.

Experts in the field of the paranormal say the best time to capture floating orbs, spirits, mists and other phenomena that are related to the supernatural, is as darkness falls over the cemeteries. From about 8 P.M. until midnight, depending on the lunar cycle, are hours that enthusiasts have reported capturing images in their camera lens. Digital cameras are said to do a better job, simply because they are capable of photographing with little or no light.

Reverence is suggested when hunting ghosts in cemeteries. Loud voices and chit-chat tend to keep spirits away, according to those who profess to know about cemetery spirits.

In the right circumstances, it is said, spirits might follow groups through the cemetery, but they don't seem to often follow people out of the confines of the burial grounds.

Somewhat to the contrary are the stories about the old cemetery on State Road 44 in Eustis, FL. It has been the location of reported sightings of a female wearing a lace outfit, walking down the side street of the cemetery. The image is so realistic that travelers have stopped to see if she needed help. But they reported that when they stopped, they heard crying in the distance, then saw the ghostly figure draped over a tombstone in the cemetery proper.

The Shadow Behind You--

In Jay, in the Florida panhandle, at the Coon Hill Cemetery, folks claim they are sometimes pushed around the cemetery by unseen hands. The sound of singing by a small child has often been reported, as well.

In Manatee County, FL a field trip taken by Barry Miller, his sister, Cherita Null, friend, Cindy Tanner to old cemeteries yielded some interesting results. They visited three cemeteries on March 31, 2006. In two of them, they encountered some definite activity. And remarkably, neither left the confines of the vehicle in which they traveled.

This was the second trip for Miller and Tanner. They had gone out a week earlier.

"We were just cruising, taking a dry run and trying out the new electromagnetic field finder, that we just acquired," said Miller.

Miller said he and his friend really didn't expect to get any reaction from the equipment, nor did they expect to capture anything in the digital camera each of them carried. He might have been classified as a "non-believer" at this juncture.

"What a shock!" Miller exclaimed. "At one spot, the meter just went wild and both of us took pictures with two different cameras and we got some absolutely fantastic photos," he added.

Miller admitted he had never really believed in the paranormal before.

"I now definitely know there is something out there," he said.

Rather sheepishly he admitted he and his friend stayed in the automobile because they were somewhat hesitant to enter the cemetery.

The two Manatee County cemeteries – one in Palmetto, FL and the other in Parrish, FL, were both established in the 1800's.

In Parrish, some of the renown names familiar to historians in the central west coast Florida area, have been laid to rest.

Energy streaks were pictured in the vicinity of the graves of Mary O. Morgan, who was buried there in 1996; and three members of the Wakeland family, Ralph, Frances M., and Pius Wakeland, all of whom were born in late 1800s or early 1900 and died in the 1920s and 1959s..

Dozens of graves for former shakers and movers in the development of the early Manatee County, are in the Parrish facility.

They continued a few miles up the road to the Palmetto Cemetery. Here, they seemed to have been met with enthusiasm by beings hovering above the grave sites.

"When we looked at the frames, we saw a photo with one or two orbs in it. The next frame pictured a couple dozen orbs near a tree that was some distance from us," Miller said.

"The third next frame, we were literally surrounded by these orbs and our electronic meter was going like crazy," he continued.

The three frames were snapped one after the other, he explained.

He said neither he nor Tanner remembered feeling any particular sensations, so both were extremely surprised when they got back to his home and looked at the photos on his computer.

"Wow! I sure didn't expect to see that," he exclaimed. "It was like they realized they had company and were coming to meet us."

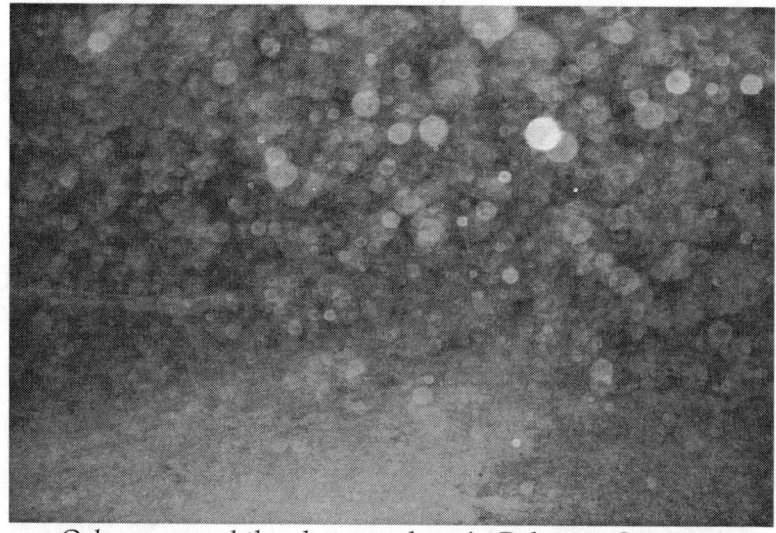

Orbs surround the photographers in Palmetto Cemetery

On the second visit, when Tanner and Miller were accompanied by Null, the three got out of the vehicle and wandered through both the Parrish and the Palmetto cemetery. There was absolutely no activity in Parrish, except for a cold reading on the Inferred laser thermometer they had with them. At Palmetto, on a hand full of orbs were photographed, in the same location where Miller and Tanner had been met by the hordes of orbs.

On subsequent visits to the Parrish Cemetery, however, Miller and Tanner encountered some shaky situations. On one trip, they picked up a reading of 26 degrees on their inferred laser thermometer. They decided to follow it. It seemed to lead them toward the back of the cemetery – a situation that Savannah historian Robert Edgerly says one should never allow himself to get into.

When Miller and Tanner reached the last row of the rural cemetery, they decided they should not continue.

A wise move, Edgerly says. He warns, "A person should never follow something that appears to be leading, or directing that person to a certain destination."

"You could open a real can of worms that way," he added.

Photos taken while Miller and Tanner followed the coldness yielded a single orb that moved along in front of them.

A couple of weeks later, Miller and Tanner, who seemed unable to resist the mystery of the cold streak, returned to the cemetery. Heeding Edgerly's advice, they stayed near their vehicle this time.

Lo and behold, their cold streak came to them.

"We picked it up at a distance, just as we had before, but we stayed where we were," Miller recalled.

Imagine their surprise and unease when the thermometer tracked the spot, which was decidedly coming closer.

"It came up and stopped right in front of us. It really shook us up," Miller recalls. "It hung out right by us for a while. We didn't know what to do, so we decided to try to talk to it. We were sort of scared, he admitted.

They could tell they had company for a few minutes, then they knew the cold spot was moving away from them.

"It started traveling back in the direction it came," he said. As it left them, they were able, with the naked eye, to see the energy streaks that mingled with the cold spot. One streak seemed to encircle a tree."

With their digital camera, they captured the streaks, but Miller said the photograph, this time, was not as impressive as what they actually witnessed.

"I don't know what that was, but it sure was something," Miller exclaimed.

Realizing the doubters might explain Miller's and Tanner's phenomena as a quirk of the camera, something in the atmosphere, or some other logical situation, they used two separate cameras at all times.

"We also visited the cemetery where we photographed the activity three consecutive times and took photos in the same locations," he said.

"At one visit, we'd get activity and another time, none. We weren't sure ourselves what was going on, so we tested it thoroughly. We still don't know what was going on, but we definitely know something was there, he declared.

Tanner and Miller also visited an old cemetery in Palm View, FL, where a school had been built next to the cemetery. They were not allowed to enter the cemetery, but they took photos along the fence separating the school and the burial ground. One of the photos showed a large congregation of orbs gathered at the fence on the cemetery side.

"Just as if they were looking through and over the fence," Miller said.

Unlike the more historic area of the United States, this mid-state area has not yet become the tour-inundated place that is seen in St. Augustine and other parts of the country.

Perhaps, then, Manatee County's ghosts are anxious for some social life; thus the reason the orbs seemed to welcome Miller and Tanner into their midst. And then again, perhaps not. Maybe they had been perfectly happy having been left alone all these years, and aren't too thrilled about all this new notoriety.

The Shadow Behind You--

Energy Bar captured in cemetery photograph

Energy streak. Brightness on limb unexplained

The Shadow Behind You--

Three different sized orbs float above multiple energy bars. The thickest of the bars were seen streaking by with the naked eye. Others captured on camera

Orbs hover behind fence between cemetery and school

The Smokey Mountains area suffered wars, diseases, fires and trouble following establishment of settlements generations ago, just as other areas did. And the early settlers, like other areas, had a lot of its dead to bury in official and non-official burial grounds.

In Cades Cove, in the heart of the Great Smokey Mountain Forest, the old 18th and 19th century churches have been preserved and are open to the public daily. Each of the churches have their own burial ground.

You won't get any of the staff to admit it, but rumor has it that most of the churches and the cemeteries in this wild preserve are haunted.

The Methodist Church is said to have an angelic spirit within its walls. Started in 1823 when Methodist circuit riders visited the pioneer families living in Cades Cove, the church has seen many uses. First services were in homes in the cove until a log meeting house was built in 1840 and became the home of the cove Methodists.

Throughout the 1800s the Methodists and the Primitive Baptists and the Missionary Baptists, which also have churches in the cove, joined together for large revivals. And some of the Baptists shared the building for church services, as well.

In 1902 the church which stands today and like the other churches in Cades Cove, the faithful congregation worshiped in the cove from its earliest years until the community ceased to exist.

But, some wonder, did one of the many traveling ministers remain in the church when it stopped holding services?

Joyce Haun, who lives in Gatlinburg, told the story about a friend who one day came into the art gallery where she works with a handful of pictures.

"He spread them out on my desk and asked me what I saw in them," she recalled. There were several photographs of the inside of the Methodist Church and at the pulpit stood a man with wings, she said. And in one of the pews there was a beautiful blond lady who also had wings.

"Honest!" she declared.

The Shadow Behind You--

Joyce's friend said he simply took a photograph of the inside of the building and when the photos were developed, there were the people who he did not see inside.

Another friend of Haun – a state trooper – visited the gallery a few days later and the photographs were still on her desk.

"Where were those pictures taken?" he asked her.

When she told him, he said he thought that was location and related a story of his early morning visit to the church and cemetery. He said as he was leaving the church and heading for the adjacent cemetery, he saw three lovely blond ladies all dressed in white.

"Then he heard voices singing and he said there were a host of voices. He said it was the most beautiful music he had ever heard," said Haun.

"I believe in angels and I think those were heavenly beings," Haun said.

Cades Cove Methodist Church. Do Angels live here?

PERHAPS NOT ALL OF THE CEMETERY RESIDENTS ARE RESTING QUIETLY

In Savannah, cemeteries are as much a part of the ghost scene as the old buildings said to be occupied by spirits. The City of Savannah today owns and operates five municipal cemeteries, but actually, the city itself could be classified as a cemetery, what with the history of death and destruction that often necessitated instant burial grounds.

It seems the paranormal stories connected to cemeteries more times than not, portray unhappy spirits and ghosts.

Savannah has several cemeteries, but two are the most visited by ghost tour groups, and both have their share of spirits and ghosts that appear to be not resting in peace. Perhaps this is because of the upheaval that left uncharted burial grounds behind in the development of the city.

Bonaventure, originally a private cemetery is located on the historical Bonaventure Plantation and has been owned by the city since 1907.

Colonial Cemetery, one of the most historic cemeteries in Savannah, opened in 1750, and closed in 1850. As early as this cemetery was originated, it still was not the first. From 1733 to 1750, colonists were buried in a cemetery on Wright Square and lies beneath a high-rise building.

A favorite dueling ground helped fill the now full Colonial cemetery. Button Gwinnett, one of the three Georgia signers of the Declaration of Independence, was killed in a duel less than a year after the signing. The famous historian died two days after being shot by his foe, Lachlin McIntosh. Today, the brightest memorial in Colonial Cemetery belongs to Gwinnett. McIntosh, who left town in disgrace, but still alive, went on to become a war hero, having fought with Washington at Valley Forge. After he died, he was buried in the Colonial as well.

The unofficial burial grounds are everywhere in Savannah.

"I hope you don't mind standing on graves," announced Wayne Lee, a guide for the "Hauntings Tour of Savannah," as he started his night tour from Bull and York Streets in the historical district. Following a dramatic pause, he continued, "Because just about anywhere you go in Savannah, you are going to be walking on someone's grave."

He explains, "Savannah was built on the dead," from the first settlers who reportedly spread Native American bones throughout the city, when it made use of the Indian mounds to fill in the low, marshy land. A city suffering tragedy upon tragedy, Savannah has many cemeteries: some legal and some not so legal, and some from which the dead were simply never removed from their original sites as the city grew on top of early burial grounds.

Savannah cemeteries were built on the edge of the early settlement. As the colony grew into a port city, the cemeteries were absorbed and homes and businesses were built on former burial sites, he explained.

Sometimes the dead were moved. Sometimes they weren't. Sometimes old cemeteries are found only when construction takes place on an old site.

Colonial Park Cemetery is one of Lee's major tour locations. Supposedly the site of many unlucky duelers, as well as those who were victims of fires, pestilence and destruction, Colonial is a favorite of the tours in the historic city.

Lee weaves tales about those who have gone on before, but seem not to be content to stay inactive. He tells stories about previous visitors who claim to have had unearthly encounters there, and also recites folklore about early residents of the inactive resting place to his tour charges.

"There are a lot of stories from this old cemetery," he said.

James Caskey, the touring company owner and author of "Haunted Savannah; the Official Guidebook to Savannah Haunted History Tour," said his growing belief in the spirit world was further fortified as a result of an event that was experienced in a cemetery by one of his guides who handled the touring duties on the night of the premier of his book.

The guide reported that two of the tour participants had spotted a woman in a nightgown in the old Colonial Park Cemetery.

"What's with the lady in the nightgown?" they asked.

"What lady in the nightgown?" countered the guide.

"The one that roamed off behind one of the gravestones," was the answer.

There was no ready answer to the question and no one else seemed to have seen the apparition.

Some time after this, the tour guide was approached by a psychic who told him "Anna" had been trying to contact him.

"When was that?" he asked. The psychic gave him the date and it turned out to be the same night the of visitors' witnessing the appearance of the lady in the cemetery.

While he had had some former experience with the supernatural, Caskey said he was still doubtful, but "that did it for me." He adds he has had many experiences with the supernatural since that time.

Colonial Park Cemetery, home to a number of shooting victims, is said to have been the site where mass graves were dug during Savannah's disease ravaged years. In the 1800's there were so many deaths from Yellow Fever that there was no time or energy to bury them in single graves. Adding to the tragic epidemic, a major fire also occurred during that same time period, destroying nearly 500 homes, and killing many other residents.

An ironic tale concerning the cemetery has it that a Savannah maid, getting off work, spotted an interesting young man. Thinking she might like to meet him, she followed him as far as the gates of the cemetery. Imagine her distress when, as she watched, he strolled through the gates and his image simply floated away.

Cemeteries are an important part of the ghost scene in St. Augustine, as well.

The Shadow Behind You--

"A Ghostly Experience" manager Pallas tells his tour group about the mysterious events of St. Augustine's cemeteries. Like Savannah, St. Augustine has both official and unofficial burial grounds.

"That building is sitting on top of an ancient cemetery," Pallas said, pointing to one of St. Augustine's historic facilities. In his deep voice he intones tales about bones being dug up from time to time during construction.

On his riding tour, Pallas doesn't delve into specific stories about cemeteries.

"I could tell you lots of stories about cemeteries, but then anybody can tell stories about cemeteries," he said, adding that guests are urged to stroll through any of St. Augustine's active cemeteries while they visit the city, and "if you feel a draft, or something brushes against you, don't be too alarmed. It's probably just one of the friendly residents of the cemetery welcoming you," he says.

"But if, while walking around the town, you feel something crunching under foot, remember that most of this town is practically a former cemetery," he recites in his resonant baritone. He, too, tells about the Indian mounds, and burials of casualties of the wars, and spins some yarns about mass grave sites that have been unearthed during building programs in St. Augustine.

The City of St. Augustine owns seven cemeteries. There are burial grounds that date back to the days before Ponce de Leon's arrival in search of the Fountain of Youth. Its history extends back into so many eras that it is as natural a place as anywhere to conjure up stories of long-gone Native Americans, slaves, Spanish, French, British and American soldiers, early settlers, or what have you who seem to be connected to the real world even after their demise. Some of them are reported as seemingly content to drift through the cemetery grounds, but many appear to be disturbed, and some seem to be downright distraught.

Former participants of "A Ghostly Experience" tours have shared photos they took while visiting St. Augustine. In a scrap book in the tour office, near the Old City gates just off St. George Street, are

The Shadow Behind You--

dozens of pictures showing orbs dancing through the tombstones of various cemeteries, with a note by the photo-taker declaring where and when the photos were taken.

Robert Samuels, a former ghost tour guide, told of what he perceives as the mischievousness of a youngster named James, who is buried in the Tolomata Cemetery on Cordova Street.

Samuels said he has heard children report having seen James, dressed in a suit, jacket and little tie, wearing a Buster Brown hair cut, up in the old live oak tree near his grave stone.

On one of his tours, he was telling the group about James. The group was near the youngster's grave and a lady in the group called, "James, if you are here, make your presence known."

"And she fell. She was standing perfectly still and down she went," Samuels recalled. She wasn't hurt, just embarrassed, and the tour group speculated on the cause of the incident. Was it James the made the lady fall? "Maybe", was the unanimous conclusion of the tour group.

Two weeks later, "in the exact same spot, I was telling the group that night about James and about the fall of the lady on the previous tour, when suddenly, a lady in that night's group fell," he declared.

"Then, so help me, the third night, I was telling the group about the two previous events, when a couple passed by us. They were not a part of the group, but as they passed the cemetery near James' grave, the man suddenly tripped and fell."

"What do I think? I think young James was up to some pranks and caused those three spills," Samuels declares, adding, "mind you, I was a skeptic when I first started the tours."

He says many of his tour participants have reported seeing apparitions, particularly in the old burial grounds.

"Since my back was always to the cemetery while I was talking to the group, I never saw anything, but I've had many reports of the heavy chain around the Tolomata swaying back and forth," he recalls.

The Tolomato Cemetery, located on Cordova Street, near the tourist-friendly St. George Street, is said to be home to other spiritual beings, as well. The Bridal Ghost is one seen often. The lady in the long white dress has been known to frighten youthful nighttime visitors to the cemetery, and has been "seen" standing behind tour guides as they told their group about the history of the Catholic burying ground. But The Bridal Ghost has also been given a more spiritual label as a guardian angel that has been reported appearing to watch over people in need of comfort.

The ghost of a Franciscan missionary, Father Corpa, has reportedly been seen by several visitors to the Tolomato Cemetery. The priest, after publicly chastising one of his Indian converts, history says, was murdered on the cemetery grounds, which at the time was an Indian village. The black-robed figure in the cemetery, therefore, was surmised to be the ghost being seen by tourists from time to time.

A few blocks away is the Huguenot Cemetery, which also seems to become active at night.

A one-time Huguenot "dweller," Judge John Stickney, who moved to St. Augustine shortly after the Civil War, is said to be roaming around the grounds, even though his family in Washington, DC had his remains relocated from St. Augustine to DC 21 years after his interment. When cemetery staff exhumed the judge's body, they found to their dismay that while the body was well preserved, grave robbers had taken his gold teeth.

Is he looking for his missing teeth?

The judge is said to have been seen sitting on a tree limb, as well and after the limb he was most often seen on took a tumble during a windstorm, he was seen on a limb higher up in the tree. There was also a report of his sitting under a tree, in a tree with a very sad countenance.

Folklore? Or history? Tour guides claim these stories are history. They are repeated over and over again, and sometimes, it is said, tour group members ask about the apparition before the tour guide gets to the story about it. Once, a small girl reported being frightened because she saw a woman standing behind the tour guide.

Historically, both the St. Augustine cemeteries have their place in history books. The Hugeunot Cemetery was established in the 1800's as a result of a yellow fever epidemic. There were no protestant churches in the predominantly Catholic settlement at the time and the victims of the fever, many from far away areas, could not be buried in the existing cemetery. Interred far from their loved ones, the Hugeunot residents may have real reason for their restlessness.

Both St. Augustine and Savannah are reported to have many cemeteries that are not only unofficial, but are unknown, until construction takes place on the site of the old resting places. Bones are often unearthed by land developers who are preparing sights for building projects.

In other southern cemeteries, ghost hunters are silently slipping through the night in hopes their cameras will capture an orb, and reports go on an on about strange sights in old and sometimes remote cemeteries. And there are a few stories about strange events in newer cemeteries that are located in the hustle and bustle of everyday activities.

DIFFERENT OPINIONS – DIFFERENT STORIES

Lurking behind the smile of many of the southern natives is the belief that as sure as they walk the street, things really do go bump in the middle of the night; and sometimes they bump around during the day time, too. And many believe those bumps are restless beings who are not yet ready to leave their earthly homes.

Ghost doubters, like David Nolan of St. Augustine, believe those bumps have a very logical origin and are not supernatural at all.

Georgia historian, Robert Edgerly, says without a doubt, his native town of Savannah, as well as lots of other towns in the United States, is very haunted and he claims history backs up his beliefs. He says stories about beings who linger behind are not folklore. They are history.

Just as there are many different theories on whether or not ghosts really do exist, there also are different theories on the "facts" of a particular ghost story. A half dozen people, all telling the same ghost story, make it sound like a half dozen different stories.

Take, for instance, stories about some of Savannah's famous ghosts and ghost residences.

"Hauntings Tours" guide, Lee tells stories he says he has heard since childhood, but stops short of declaring himself a true believer in the paranormal. Mirthfully, he will tell you he's never seen a ghost, but knows people who say they have.

"Legend has it," is a favorite phrase for Lee.

The young Lee leds a fast-paced 90-minute walk through Savannah's narrow streets one fall night recently. He took the would-be ghost hunters to many of the haunts of Savannah, and "believer" or not, he had dozens of scary stories to tell about each of his ghostly locations.

At Wright Square, once the site of Savannah's hanging gallows, as well as the early cemetery, Lee looks up among the branches and tells his followers that this is not only the site of Savannah's hanging gallows, but the site of the first woman to be hanged…ever.

He told of the old courthouse that was located adjacent to Wright Square. He went on to describe the hanging gallows that were located in the middle of the square.

With the flair of a campfire story teller, Lee painted an eerie tale about Alice Riley, a poor Irish indentured servant of an unsavory character, William Wise. It was Wise's habit to order his servants to bathe and wash his waist-long hair. It became the job of Alice Riley and the man historians claim was her husband, Richard White, to groom the mean-spirited man. As Wise lay on his bed, White would comb the freshly washed hair, while Riley bathed him.

"He was one mean man!" Lee believes. He mistreated his servants in the worst possible way, he explained.

"They grew pretty tired of being mistreated and conspired to kill him," Lee related. "They held his head in the pail of water used for his bathing, until he drowned," he added.

He told a detailed story about how Alice, first woman to be hanged, died a tormented death that took days, as she hung on the gallows, moaning and gasping for breath.

"And to this day, people say they can still hear her gasping and see her petticoats swaying among the tree branches," he concludes, leaving his tour participants sneaking furtive glances upward into the tree just in case Alice is watching them.

"She won't be there now. She hates crowds. Come back at midnight, alone, and you may see her," Lee instructs, adding in an undertone, "and a couple of shots at your favorite pub probably won't hurt, either."

Edgerly puts a less dramatic slant on the Alice Riley story. He agrees that she and her husband, Richard White, indeed devised a way to kill their boss by pushing his head under the water in the bucket Alice used for washing his hair. After the drowning, the couple fled Savannah.

"But they caught them and Richard White was hung immediately," declared Edgerly.

The Shadow Behind You--

Edgerly continues to explain that Alice was pregnant and the authorities weren't going to hang a woman with child. So they threw her in the stockade and left her there until her baby was born.

Even after the child was born, there was a problem with hanging Alice on the public gallows, he continued. Officials weren't anxious to have her on public display for three days.

In an effort to keep away the "sight-seers" who wandered around the gallows area during public hangings, the hangmen placed a rope high in the treetops of the near-by oak tree and hanged her among the branches. Only her feet and petticoats were visible from the ground and then, only if the individual was willing to look way up.

Lee tells a dramatic tale of Alice's imprisonment in the stockade and subsequent final trip to the hanging tree. He describes her agonizing punishment and says the loud gasping for breath and moans continued for 72 hours, before she was declared dead as a result of having been hung by the neck.

Edgerly said he believes that since Alice was poor, she probably didn't get a very kind hangman. People condemned to die on the gallows were able, in the 1800's to pay the hangman for a speedy death. Those unable to pay, usually suffered a long, slow death, he explained.

This is not just a ghost story, Edgerly says. It is history. "And there is nothing new under the sun."

And indeed, this story of the crime was an historical event, recorded in historical documents. The different stories about Alice's suffering and her late night re-appearances in the tree from which she was hung could also be history. Or it could be folklore? Or the product of a healthy imagination?

Caskey, the "Savannah's Haunted History Tour" owner, says historical records put the date of this happening at March, 1734 when the pair put an end to the mistreatment by Wise.

But Caskey's dates of the executions disagree with those provided by Edgerly and Lee. Casky, in his book, places the date of Alice's execution at January 19, 1735, 10 months after the alleged murder, a date that is mutually agreed upon. He does however disagree with the idea that White preceded her in death. He says White was hanged on January 20, 1735, a day after Alice's death.

The baby born to Alice was healthy at birth, but died 45 days later, of pneumonia, Edgerly said.

There's also some mild disagreement on Alice's true crime. Some say she was put to death for practicing witchcraft. Others claim she cursed the Savannah officials, causing her to be hanged by the neck.

Just like an automobile accident, when seven witnesses offer seven testamonies on the event, seven story tellers have seven different versions on some historical or fabled facts.

Edgerly is absorbed in the historical value of the city, and has many ghost stories to tell—most of them true, but perhaps, in his lighter moments, some, possibly folklore.

He declares that Savannah's heritage demands the presence of ghostly beings. The Scottish, Irish and English that settled here, came with the ingrained superstition of their homelands. There were Native Americans, slaves, pirates, warriors, and other people bent on killing, or being killed, in the early settlement.

"There are a lot of ghosts from all of these elements and mix them with Voodoo and the Native American lore, and that almost assures us of having some paranormal activity here," he said.

Savannah was the battleground of one of the greatest battles ever fought. Today's Chippewa Square was the site of the second bloodiest battle of the Revolutionary War.

Sitting in the Six Pence Pub on Bull Street, Edgerly told of the many reports of paranormal activity within the confines of the popular bar and restaurant. Staff and patrons alike, have shared stories about the experiences they have had with ghostly beings.

He gestured toward the floor of the vintage building and told of the two basements – one built on the top of the other. He said the most subterranean, he believed, was connected to the old British military barracks, which were located across the street.

"There's a drunken British soldier who lives down there," he proclaimed. "He has scared many people who ventured into the basement. He sometimes appears on the stairs and gives some of the people – the ladies in particular – a scare," he added.

Edgerly believes the soldier may have been on duty in the sub-basement, which may have been part of the magazine storage for the military barracks.

"He probably was drunk, since standing guard in such dank and dreary quarters is not a job most folks would desire," Edgerly surmises. "He was probably killed while on duty and doesn't know he's dead yet," he continued in a perfectly sincere tone.

Six Pence is noteworthy in modern history, because it was portrayed as the site of betrayal by the husband of the character played by Julia Roberts in "Something to Talk About."

The Shadow Behind You--

SOME NOTED SPIRITS IN SAVANNAH

One of the most famous ghosts of Savannah is "Anna" who was reportedly jilted by her lover and is said to await his return in the "honeymoon suite," Room 204, of the 17Hundred90 Inn and Restaurant. This quaint inn and restaurant, one of the oldest operating establishments in Savannah was actually built in 1820, but some think there is evidence that it was built over an earlier building which may actually have been built in 1790.

Anna is perpetually pining for her lover and, according to Lee, "people staying overnight in room 204 are often awakened by her tears falling gently on their faces."

Reports of overnight guests feeling a feminine presence are numerous and some report of having items, especially dainty feminine items, go missing while they stay in the room. Some are apparently not to "Anna's" liking, since they reappear in strange, and sometimes embarrassing, places, the young tour guide proclaims.

Lee tells a comical tale about a couple staying in Room 204, and how while the man lay on the bed awaiting his wife who was preparing for the night in another part of the suite, was frightened so badly by Anna, that he crawled under the bed.

Lee claims the man's wife, upon her entry to the bedroom, found her husband huddled under the bed and had to call for help from the front desk to get him out.

"When that man was finally coaxed from beneath that bed, he was so frightened, he refused to stay in that room another minute," the tour story-teller relates to his charges.

"He fled down the sidewalk to the sister inn across the street, wearing only his underclothes" while carrying his outer garments wadded in his arms, Lee says.

The latter part of Lee's tale may be an embellishment.

Edgerly tells the same story, but his source, staff members of the facility, say they simply calmed the shaken man down, then moved he and his wife to an adjoining room of the inn.

He said that guests have reported encountering Anna, who is usually weeping wherever she is seen.

"I haven't heard that story before of the man in his underwear," commented Lisa Gallagher, manager of the restaurant.

However, Lisa does have some stories of her own.

One of them involves Sean Dunbrook, an employee of the restaurant/inn whose job it was to pick up breakfast orders from the rooms upstairs. He experienced several fearsome events and now refuses to near Room 204. He tells of feeling a presence was watching him as he collected the tickets from door knobs on the second floor. Then, as he approached room 204, he reports he was lifted six inches off the floor by something that had grasped him by his elbows. Like any red-blooded man, he ran. As fast as his feet would take him. He attempted one other time to enter the room, when the Travel Channel film crew asked him to reenact the occurrence. He found it impossible to enter the room. He said he was blocked by some unseen barricade.

There is disagreement over how Anna left her earthly life, as well. Some say she plunged to her death when she jumped off her second-floor balcony outside her room in the 17Hundred90 Inn, landing in the brick courtyard below, as her lover's ship sailed out to sea. Others say she was murdered by an unloving husband. "Believers" agree, however, that Anna is a ghostly resident of the Inn. Some have reported seeing her on the porch of the building and others reported mysterious rocking of the chairs on the porch. Sounds and sights of opening doors and windows are also among the ghostly tales about Anna.

The 17Hundred80 Restaurant and Inn is home to other paranormal beings, Lisa says. There's Tizzy, the deceased former cook, who was deeply into voodoo, and is said to visit the kitchen regularly. She makes her presence known by throwing things around.

Kelly, the cook on duty during our discussion, said Tizzy doesn't seem to like her at all.

"She throws plates and pans at me," Kelly says.

There's also a mischievous little boy who reportedly runs around the restaurant blowing out candles, and playing ball, as well as the old fellow in civil war era garments, who drops in to listen to Jack the piano player.

Lisa, who arrived at the restaurant four years ago without a single belief in the paranormal, had an experience which changed her mind. One night, she was reaching for the light switch, which was just out of her grasp. As she was about to seek something to stand on, the light went out. The switch had been turned off, apparently by someone tall enough to reach it. She swears it is too high for just anyone to reach.

"I'd heard about Savannah's ghosts, and there was just no other explanation for that light being turned off, so I just said 'thank you' and continued my closing chores," she recalled.

Lisa Gallagher speaks with author inside the "haunted" restaurant/Inn in Savannah

The Shadow Behind You--

LOTS OF TALES IN HAUNTED SAVANNAH

The 1822 house, which was the birthplace of Juliette Gordon Low, may be the most haunted in Savannah.

Low, founder of the Girl Scouts in America, was born on Halloween night in 1860 in the house, which today is the headquarters for the scouting organization and often is temporary home for scout groups visiting the city. Family diaries allude to the haunting of the house, and police have been called to it numerous times, because of a suspected haunting intruder.

William Gordon, a general in the U. S. Army who served both in the Civil and the Spanish-American wars was born in the house. He brought his wife Nellie to live in the house. He took ill and promised his distraught wife he would return to her upon her death. Upon her death years later, her five grown children were with her when she died, and according to writings about the death, William was on hand to welcome her into the ethereal life.

Legend has it, said Lee, the spirit of Nellie Gordon, Low's mother, walks around in the home frequently, even though she died in 1917.

Adding to the eeriness of the house is the fact that history reports the house sits on top of Savannah's first burial ground. And the spirits beneath that house are said to roam the grounds regularly.

Hampton Lillibridge house, owned by the late Jim Williams, a Georgia antique dealer who was tried three times for the murder of his associate Danny Hansford, is prominently on every tour route in Savannah. The movie, "Midnight in the Garden of Good and Evil" was inspired by the house owners' trials and acquittal for the heinous crime. Tour guides regale visitors with hair-raising tales about the spirits that are said to have haunted this structure.

It was reported to be so haunted, that during its renovation, Williams was hard pressed to keep workers on the job. When finally the construction work was completed and Williams moved into the house, there were so many reports to police of unexplained happenings, that the department's chief threatened to start charging

The Shadow Behind You--

for "false alarms." However, legend has it, that while an officer was at the house explaining the rule set forth by the chief, an old piano (not a player piano) began playing a tune by unseen hands, which cast some doubts on the part of the policeman that the reports of the hauntings were false.

Finally, Williams contracted an Episcopal bishop to perform an exorcism on the house, which seemed to have calmed the spirits for a while.

Today, the Hampton Lillibridge house is a "must see" among tourists attractions in Savannah.

There are some ghostly tales surrounding the Richardson-Owens-Thomas house in Savannah. There's general agreement that the house is haunted, but the identity of the supernatural being is questioned. Some see a lady ghost, while others are sure there's gentleman who occupies the old house today. In truth, it is not even a real residence anymore.

Designed by William Jay and bequeathed to the Telfair Academy in 1951 by Miss Margaret Thomas, the mansion stands at Abercorn and President Streets, facing Oglethorpe Square. Built in 1818, the Regency style house has been featured in several books dealing with haunted places.

Before it became today's museum, it was home for a relative of Jay, Richard Richardson, a banker and cotton merchant. It also was at one time, a prestigious boarding house operated by Mary Maxwell. It was also the spacious home for Sen. George Owens, congressman and former mayor of Savannah.

It was the place that Margaret Thomas was born and the place where she died. In the same bedroom, in the same bed, historians tell us. And it is the place where her spirit still dwells, ghost enthusiasts say.

The appearance of having rounded corners, and other architectural oddities, makes the Owens-Thomas House unique. But inside the spacious early 19th century house are other surprises. There was running water in the bathrooms, as well as other modern technology. The thick walls are constructed of tabby.

The Shadow Behind You--

Tour Guide Lee says, the rounded corners were Jay's effort to keep ghosts away. But, says Lee, it didn't work. He claims the Owens Thomas house is most definitely haunted. The ghost he heard most about was Miss Thomas, but others talk about male ghosts as well.

Lee claims that Miss Thomas was a lady who liked to give parties, and "Miss Thomas continues to throw some gala affairs, even though she died many years ago," he said. He went on to explain that people staying in near-by guest houses report having been awakened in the middle of the night by loud voices and music. When they peered out their windows, they saw a lone lady in white.

"The theory about the rounded corners is nonsense," exclaimed Edgerly, although he quickly admits there have been sightings of ghosts at the house. He said he had heard a report from Jim Williams, the businessman who was tried four times for the murder and was still found "not guilty" and was made famous in "Murder in the Garden of Good and Evil." He thought he had seen Sen. Owens in the house.

Both Edgerly and Casky are convinced the house is occupied by the spirit world, but both said they had never heard of the lady hostess being seen in the party mode at the home.

"Miss Owens loved to have gatherings with her friends alright, but I've never heard of her giving ghostly parties," Edgerly said.

Caskey disputes the legend that the house has rounded corners to dispel ghosts.

"It's the Regency Style and it has nothing to do with superstition," Caskey said..

The rounded corners were a key characteristic of this style, he said. False doors, the rounded entry door, a set of winding stairs, and a room that is actually square but made to look round with mirrors, and clever visual tricks, are all quirks used in this architectural style, according to Caskey.

Caskey tells of tales of a ghostly being which appeared to two men who were visiting a friend in the upstairs apartments of the Owens-Thomas House.

Although the tenant saw nothing amiss during the visit, the two visitors swore they saw a man in a riding coat and a shirt with ruffles who stood in the doorway, then passed through a wall into another room.

Staff members have reported strange rearrangement of furniture in the house.

One of Savannah's tour guides, according to Lee, was regaling her tour group with some tales about the house, and as she was talking outside the mansion, she smelled cigar smoke. She didn't see anyone smoking, but when she asked group members if they smelled smoke, several members of the group said not only had they smelled smoke, they had seen the light of a match flare up.

Imposing front entrance of the Owen Thomas House, said to house unearthly residents

There are different opinions on identity and activities of the ghost, or ghosts who live in the William Kehoe House, the lovely home of the Kehoe family. Built in 1892, this Renaissance Revival

The Shadow Behind You--

house which has cast iron on all outside trim and columns, today is a bed and breakfast. It's had many owners, including Joe Namath, during its 100-plus year reign. A funeral home occupied the stately house for many years after the Kehoe family departed.

Today, listed in the National Registry, the house is a charming Victorian Bed and Breakfast, and has a long waiting list of prospective visitors who apparently have a keen desire to "sleep with a ghost."

Lee claims that the ghost of Mrs. Kehoe, a particularly overbearing woman, still lives in the house. And she still practices some of the mean pranks she did as an earthly mother bent on controlling her family. Sometimes, Lee says, she gets so worked that people with small children are advised not to stay at the home until Mrs. Kehoe finishes venting.

She made all of her children---and legend says there were many of them—move back into the house so "she could keep track of what they did," Lee said.

Her passion, he continued, other than "ruling the family with an iron hand," was to creep into the halls in the dead of night, hurl a heavy object down the stairs while screaming "manically." This, of course, brought her frantic children and their families bolting into the hall to check on the clatter.

Lee swears people who have stayed in the bed and breakfast are often awakened by objects falling down the stairs and, in addition, they have reported hearing what sounded like a child crying, leading them to believe a child has fallen down the stairs. Lee says folks believe it is the dominating mother still playing her pranks.

Edgerly agrees the sound of a child crying has been reported. It is believed the crying stems from the fact that several of the Kehoe babies didn't survive, and the crying children may be the ghosts of those children. He also says he has a friend who saw a lady in white in the house. The friend had worked in the Kehoe House Bed and Breakfast for four years and never saw anything unusual. Then, in August, 2000, she saw a "shade" Edgerly said.

Caskey tells a story of Kehoe twins who reportedly died while playing in a chimney in one of the rooms. While the fireplaces have

The Shadow Behind You--

all been blocked up and angels have been painted on them, there are many reports of Kehoe Bed and Breakfast guests hearing children laughing and small footsteps running in the hall outside the blocked fireplace.

Another tour guide reported a child's voice begging her to play with it. Her story was backed up by the people in the tour who were astonished to hear the plaintive voice. There've been other reports of children in the house, as well.

Bill Kehoe himself has reportedly been seen gracing the premises, even though he left his earthly life many years ago.

The Kehoe House Bed and Breakfast

The Davenport House, built in 1820, boasting of double stairs leading to the majestic front entrance doors has been reported to have a child apparition living upstairs, but more noteworthy, it seems to have a feline ghost there as well. Several people have reported seeing the tabby cat lounging on the stairs, rubbing against visitor's legs and purring. Not to be confused as being a live pet, this cat, like many of his human counterparts, seems to disappear before folks' eyes, if reports of these events can be believed.

These are just a few of the historic Savannah homes that boast of having resident spirits and ghosts that mingle with guests who come to visit the elegant homes.

Throughout the country, there have been reports of haunted homes.

St. Augustine homes are said to be teeming with ghosts of years gone by, and some of the more modern day hotels in places like Gatlinburg, TN have had ghostly visitors who decided to stay. The next two chapters will give you a thumbnail sketch of places where you can "sleep with a ghost" in several locations.

Ghost history? Or folklore?

HOT COMMODITIES: GHOSTS, BED & BREAKFASTS, AND INNS

"The hottest commodities in Savannah today are ghosts, Bed and Breakfasts and inns," says Murray Silver, who rose to fame when his first book, "Great Balls of Fire: The Uncensored Story of Jerry Lee Lewis," was made into a movie. A fifth generation of Savannah, Silver has recently released "Behind the Moss Curtain – And Other Great Savannah Stories."

"I've personally encountered many of Savannah's ghosts and have captured the energy on camera," he said.

"There's a lot of energy going on in Savannah these days," he said.

"There's an excellent chance that anyone spending any time at all in this city will experience the supernatural," said Silver.

It's illegal to tear down Savannah's historic buildings, so, according to Silver, the energy that has been in them for decades just "hangs around." He believes most of Savannah's old homes have spectral activity.

"People come here from all parts of the world to take ghost tours and to sleep in bed and breakfasts that are reported to be haunted," Silver says. By staying in a bed and breakfast, instead of going to one of the big hotels, guests can be in the heart of Savannah's history and they may get an opportunity to "sleep with a ghost," Silver continued

The Kehoe House is a wonderful example of the grandness of the Bed and Breakfast offerings in Savannah. Built in 1892 by Kehoe, an Irish immigrant, the brick mansion is touted as one of the most romantic bed and breakfasts in the United States. Folks who stay there are always delighted with the luxury, but some are treated to the excitement of "pleasant, and perhaps not so pleasant, ghostly experiences."

Surrounding the many squares in Savannah are an array of graceful old mansions that have been turned into thriving bed and breakfasts, inns and other hospitality facilities. Most are, of course,

The Shadow Behind You--

said to house paranormal residents, but seldom does that deter visitors from wanting to spend a night, or more, with history and perhaps, with ghosts.

Although many ghostly frightening experiences have been reported in Room 204 of the 17Hundred Ninety Inn, there is a huge desire on the part of would-be guests to spend the night there. The waiting list is quite long.

The Marshall House in Savannah, built in 1851 and restored in 1999, offers southern hospitality and ghostly guests to visitors. Said to have housed yellow fever victims and injured soldiers during the Civil War, the stately 88-room hotel is said to be seething with spirits. Sounds of a child bouncing a ball up and down the hallways, of the little person's feet skipping along, and of a laughing youngster have been reported. This building, like the Davenport House, also seems to have a phantom cat.

Folks venturing into the Mercer House may well encounter the ghost of the famous Jim Williams who was said to be a party animal who gave lavish parties in his home on Monterey Square.

After completion of the renovation of the Hampton Lillibridge house, Williams moved into the Mercer House on Monterey Square and became well know for his huge parties.

Following his death, rumors began drifting around town that visitors had seen lights and heard the sounds of parties in the Mercer House. Yet, all was silent and no parties were taking place. These activities reportedly took place on Williams' five-year anniversary of being acquitted in the Hansford shooting. It also is the anniversary of a gala celebration he held that night, following the court action.

The Stephen Williams House on Liberty Street takes its visitors back into the 1800s with beautiful antiques throughout the eight-unit guest house. Not on the rostrum of having a resident ghost, the charming Bed and Breakfast nevertheless has a huge attraction for visitors to Savannah.

Dr. Albert Wall, co-owner with Brandon Lucas, said the lovely old home had been used as an apartment house at one time. The apartment house owners had divided the stately rooms by the least expensive method, but this, Wall said, was a good thing for him. They simply covered up all the graceful archways and lovely woodwork, and it was relatively easy to restore the home to its 19th century grandeur, he said. The new owners then turned the home into a charming bed and breakfast chock full of wonderful antiques.

Dr. Wall said he has had some prestigious visitors to the inn and commented further that the late Jim Williams, an expert on antiques, had told him that he had some of the "finest antiques" that he had ever seen displayed in the guest house.

The innkeeper also boasted about his acquaintance with Tom Hanks and his wife during the filming of "Forrest Gump" in Savannah. Rita Hanks celebrated her birthday on Wall's yacht, he said.

"I heard that she mentioned her party on the Oprah Winters show," he added, with pride.

This, and other homes built around the squares of Savannah, sit on Gen. Oglethorpe's "tithing lots" that were only 30 feet wide. This meant the owners either had to acquire more than one lot, or build tall narrow homes. It was the general's urban planning method when he helped settle the Georgia town.

Jill Smith, owner of Destination Southern Style, works closely with the hospitality industry in Savannah. An all-purpose travel agent who does everything from planning the trip, booking transportation, and reserving the hotel rooms, Jill said Savannah is awash with hospitality rooms.

She said she deals mostly with the small inns in Savannah, but has been involved in some deals with the Kehoe House, the Marshall House, the Foley House, Ye Olde Pink House, the Planter Inn and the Dresser Palmer House, all of which she says are elegant hospitality facilities. All are also reported to have some ghostly residents.

"I'm able to negotiate better rates at the hotels," she said.

If visitors don't fancy staying in a bed and breakfast or an old inn, Ron Purser, owner of "Savannah Getaways" may have the housing answer for them.

The Shadow Behind You--

Purser manages many of the old homes in the Historic District for absentee owners. He also owns several of the homes himself. Folks come in from around the country to spend a couple of nights, a week, or more, living right in the midst of history and, of course, of those unearthly beings that may have taken up residency in the ancient, but well preserved homes.

"Savannah is one of the top 10 vacation spots in the nation and the historical district is a real draw," Purser said.

Purser bought his first Historic District home in 1999 and started soliciting neighbors to join him. Before long, he was having people come to him. They saw a good thing and latched onto it. There now are 100-plus properties available for vacation rentals.

Tom Mott, a retired consultant, owns several properties that are rented through Purser's operation. One of his properties on E. Taylor Street are two 1873 townhouses in a single building. Behind them is a former artists studio that he converted into a cottage. The three units are situated around a large deck and are rented separately, or to groups, Mott said.

My husband and I stayed in the artist studio while visiting Savannah and found it to be quite charming.

In fact, although I did not acknowledge it as such, I may have had a paranormal experience in the little cottage.

The bathroom opened off the bedroom and did not offer access from any other part of the cottage. As noted, the cottage was behind the dual two-story building, and there was no view from any street of the little house. Completely fenced with a high wooden fence, it also did not have a view of any other structure in the neighborhood.

On our last morning there, I was at the bathroom mirror, with the door open, preparing to leave. Husband Ken was picking up odds and ends and packing them away. One of the items was a tiny pen flashlight that he customarily carries on all trips.

I saw a flash of light arc in the mirror and go around the walls of the bathroom. I thought that for some reason, Ken had turned on his little flashlight and it had shown through the open door and into the bathroom. However, when I came out, I found that Ken had been

The Shadow Behind You--

in another part of the cottage. My next thought was that it was light reflecting off a car, until I realized I could not have seen it, because no automobile could get close enough to the secluded cottage.

Practical person that I am, however, I dismissed the entire thing from my mind, until later in the day. Ken and I pondered the event, but didn't label it as anything paranormal. We also could not think of any source of the light.

Could it have been a ghostly farewell?

One of Mott's other properties, a two-story duplex located several blocks away on Bryan St., may have a spirit living there, Mott says.

"I haven't encountered any ghostly things at Bryan, but a couple, Janet and Wiley, stayed downstairs for about five months. They are convinced there was a ghost living above them," he said.

Janet told Mott that she heard someone walking around in the upper floor. She said it sounded like a woman's pace.

Mott told the couple that no one should be upstairs at all. His advice was to call the police, but the couple decided to set up some "traps" in an effort to catch an intruder, if somehow, the individual had been able to gain entrance through the locked door. No earthly being ever disturbed their traps, however.

On another occasion, a piece of tableware slide across the counter and landed on the floor as they sat eating in the adjoining great room. A CD left out in the great room overnight had a deposit of some kind of "slimy gelatinous stuff" on it the next morning and puddles were on the floor.

One night, from the square outside, Janet and her husband saw through the upstairs window that ceiling fan light was on. No one had been in this particular room since their stay began and it had not been on any night previously.

Mott said the couple invited a "ghost expert" who does tours and lectures in Savannah to come into the house, and he said he "felt the presence of spirits," Mott said.

A couple of other tenants who were in the downstairs apartment at another time, called Mott with a report that the porch

The Shadow Behind You--

light was on above the entrance to the foyer leading upstairs when they first approached the house. They said upon entering the foyer, they found the switch and turned the light off. They then locked the outside door from the inside using the key that was in the lock on the inside. They removed the key. The next day, the door was still locked, but the light was on again.

The Shadow Behind You--

HOSPITALITY INDUSTRY BRISK
IN ST. AUGUSTINE

Like Savannah, many of St. Augustine's old buildings today have been converted into inns or Bed and Breakfasts, restaurants and other like facilities.

Near the Tolomato Cemetery is the "Southern Wind," an inn which has been operating in a 1916 home, is said to house a resident lady ghost. Some say she may have been a bride because her apparition appears in a long flowing white dress.

Catalina's Garden, now a restaurant, but once the 1750's home of a gracious lady, named Catalina. She had been married while in Cuba, then had returned to Florida in 1783, and regained ownership of her home. The original house burned in 1887, but was rebuilt to become a series of restaurants before the current Catalina's Garden. A gentleman dressed in black has been reported seen in the downstairs portion of the restaurant. He stands around, and then passes effortlessly through walls, cabinets and other objects as he exits the room. Staff members have reported seeing another apparition – this one a lady – upstairs. Catalina, perhaps? Some think so.

Jayne James, Innkeeper of Casablanca Inn, says her guests have reported having encountered paranormals in three of her rooms. Located on Avenida Menendez, this genteel home on the bay is touted for its romantic atmosphere. James says she has never even sensed any paranormal activity in the inn, but guests have encountered energy in at least three of the rooms. Like most of the buildings in St. Augustine, the Casablanca Inn dates back to long gone days and no doubt has seen its share of sadness and tragedy. Supposedly, James says, Rooms 9, 10, and 11 have spirits living in them.

"I can't dispute what the patrons say," James said. She's puzzled, however, since she believes she has a keen sense of the paranormal and wonders why she cannot feel the presence of her ghostly residents.

Legend has it that the Casablanca, located across the street from Manazas Bay, has a lady ghost living there. Living during the prohibition, the lady, a widow, took the role of look-out for the "Feds" for her rum-running beau and his cronies. When she spotted the officials, she would dash onto the roof of the building and would wave a lantern to warn the men.

Although the lady of the house has long been laid to rest, shrimpers and fishermen in the bay today sometimes report seeing a lantern swaying above the Casablanca Inn.

The St. Francis Inn, built in 1791, is St. Augustine's oldest inn. Visitors to this inn have reported seeing a young girl dressed in white floating down the hallway.

A boarding house until it was purchased in 1838 by a Marine's colonel, who died a year after purchasing the house. Col. Thomas Dummett's widow, in 1845, gave the home to her two daughters, Sarah and Anna. Anna again opened the home as a boarding house.

Anna's brother-in-law, Major William Hardee, assumed ownership of the house ten years later. In 1888, the house was purchased by John Wilson.

Today, the St. Francis is a modernized inn with lots of charm and no doubt, according to reports from guests, lots of spirits.

While the hospitality industry in St. Augustine is welcomed by most, there's one resident who isn't thrilled with the trend toward turning structures into places to shelter the traveler.

"Every widow who owned one of the old houses in St. Augustine turned it into an inn or a bed and breakfast and every inn and B & B had its own resident ghost," commented historian David Nolan. Critical of the mystic reputation that has been given to St. Augustine, Nolan said none of the stories about the hospitality industry ghosts have been found to be historically sound.

Different folks – different opinions.

HAUNTED INNS ELSEWHERE

Historical truth, or legend, inns have been reported as being haunted throughout the south.

In Gatlinburg, TN, a noted former inn that today is a thriving restaurant on top of a mountain on the outskirts of the tourist town. The Greenbrier Restaurant is said to be haunted by a young woman who reportedly committed suicide in the wake of seemingly being jilted at the alter.

Becky Hadden and her husband David bought the old inn/restaurant about 13 years ago. The 1914 building is impressive with a view that seems to go right off the side of the mountain through a well of floor to ceiling windows.

Hadden said there have been "encounters" with the supernatural since she and David started operating the facility.

It seems that in the late 1930's, Lydia, a young woman who lived at the then Greenbrier Lodge, was scheduled to marry a Gatlinburg gentleman.

On the day of the wedding, Lydia, in her long white dress went into town to meet her lover at the Church.

But the groom failed to show up and after several hours of waiting, Lydia returned to the lodge alone and in deep despair. Unable to fight off her anger and frustration, she climbed the stairs to the second floor landing, threw a rope over one of the rafters and hung herself by the neck. This part of the restaurant, today, is open for group meetings and special events, Hadden said.

Her lover was found dead in the Great Smokey Mountain forest, mauled by a mountain lion. Locals are convinced Lydia's spirit took on the form of a cat and sent her lover to an early grave.

Lydia's body was buried on family property near the restaurant, but for some reason her grave was not marked.

Dean Hadden, David's father, told a story about a caretaker at the lodge being awakened nightly by a plaintive cry from the spirit of Lydia imploring him to "mark my grave." After several nights of listening to the plea, the caretaker was said to have gone to the grave, cut down a small tree, made a cross and hammered it into the ground.

Hadden said the caretaker never heard her cries again.

However, guests at the restaurant have reported seeing her apparition drifting through the second floor, where her small sad figure has roamed from table to table during some of the special events that take place on that second floor.

Ghost history in the Appalachians? Or Mountain folklore?

Gatlinburg's Holiday Inn Sunspree Resort is reportedly haunted by many spirits and even has a resident demon or two.

One of the oldest hotels in the area, the inn is a center for numerous tales of supernatural encounters.

A suicide by one of the guests is said to have left behind a shadow figure that strolls around the pool at night. The murder of several boy scouts in the early 1980's, apparently left sounds of people in rooms that are vacant. A former cook was given a boat by the owners on his 30th anniversary working there. He took the boat out and it immediately sank and he drowned. Current cooks claim his spirit prowls the kitchen, breaking dishes, turning faucets on and off, and calling the kitchen staff in whispers. And the tales go on and on.

Coca colas have reportedly dropped from the hall machine when nobody was around, and the ice machine has been said to drop ice by itself. Folks have reported rearrangement of their belongings upon their return to their room, even when the staff swore no one had been in their room.

Rocky Top Inn in Gatlinburg, was the scene of a multiple murder of two motel employees. Today, staff say, screams can be heard and people see apparitions drifting around the grounds.

The Windsor Hotel in Americas, GA built in 1892, is said to have a little girl spirit who speaks in the hallway at night. Also in Americas, the Americus Garden Inn Bed & Breakfast, a pre-civil war inn, has had numerous reports of doors opening on their own, radios which turn themselves on and off, and footsteps have been heard in unoccupied rooms.

The Shadow Behind You--

We've stayed in both of these Americus structures and never had any paranormal feelings about the majestic Windsor Hotel or the more homey Americus Garden Inn.

Both are old enough to harbor spectral activity and other patrons swear they've seen and heard from these spiritual beings. Some have reportedly captured "orbs" with their cameras – especially on the grounds of the Americus Garden Inn. Innkeepers, Kim and Susan Egleseer, welcome and encourage folks interested in the paranormal to explore their lovely gardens in search for a ghostly being.

And historically, the area of Americus seems ripe for some kind of essence.

Americus is within a stone's throw of the Andersonville National Historic Site, the scene of the death of many in the Confederate Camp. In the camp, 45,000 Union troops were imprisoned and 13,000 died. This haunted place whose name over time became synonymous with the horror of death and disease, is just outside Americus, and though some experts say spirits in cemeteries never follow folks out of the confines of the burial plots, some of Americus citizenry are convinced they are visited from time to time by these ghosts of the historical past.

The 1872 John Denham House in Monticello, FL offers hands-on seminars for ghost tracking. The 130-year-old bed and breakfast which is on the National Historic Register was reported as having "Ten Places to Sleep with a Ghost," in USA Today in 2003. It is "certifiably haunted," and annually holds a ghost tracking course in concert with the International Ghost Hunter's Society.

So, if you're looking to spend the night with a ghost, you have lots of options. See for yourself if it is ghost history, or folklore?

GHOST COMMUNITY ACTIVE

Caskey, author of "The Hauntings of Savannah," who moved from Deland, Florida to Savannah to attend art school in the prestigious Savannah College of Art and Design, said he had felt the "weirdness" of Savannah, but did not accept the stories of ghostly beings wandering the streets, squares and buildings of the ancient town. He was convinced the stories he was hearing were just stories.

A caretaker job in a bed and breakfast on Tybee Island just outside the confines of Savannah turned out to be the beginning of his turning point. The bed and breakfast was housed in one of the old buildings that made up Fort Screven. His duties were during the winter months, when the inn was empty.

He told of hearing the sound of heavy boots treading the hallways at nights and of numerous incidents of locks unlocking when there was no logical way for them to be unlocked and finally, of witnessing the tubular bolt slide out of its mooring without benefit of another living soul around.

The ghost in the Fort Screven is an oft discussed legend in the area. Many tales about eerie events that took place within the bed and breakfast add zest to the image of the old inn. Such bazaar things as a lady who was reportedly held down and bitten on the neck fail to keep the tenants away. They all want to "sleep with a ghost".

History? Or folklore?

Lee can always guarantee a shiver or two when he stops his group in front of the old abandoned hospital that he said housed dying and insane soldiers, and victims of diseases that plagued Savannah.

"There's a lot of death in the history of this old hospital," Lee declares.

History books report the top floor of the hospital was a quarantine ward for half a century. It housed sailors who arrived in the port with suspected contagious diseases.

The structure is a favorite of tour guides because it often offers appearances that some paranormal activity definitely takes place within the walls of the large structure.

"Those with digital cameras always get pictures of orbs," Lee said. He spread his arms to indicate the areas they have been captured in the lens of cameras. In an area between the flag pole and the building, and inside, through some of the windows, Lee said there has been energy photographed. The half dozen or so people pointing their digital cameras toward the old building all immediately had photos of round hazy white orbs.

One of the photos showed something in a window that could have been an ethereal being.

"You stay away from me," Lee jokingly told the photographer who captured the image.

Lee said his wife is more sensitive to the paranormal than he is.

"She often sees things that I cannot see, and she can sometimes see orbs with her naked eye. She can always spot orbs here," Lee explained.

Those who are considered experts in the field of the paranormal believe some people attract ghosts to them.

"There definitely are those who are more prone to experience a paranormal event," says St. Augustine parapsychologist Harry Stafford.

A little humor was introduced along with the tales about the supernatural, as the tour group strolled in front of the old hospital. As the group passed one of the last windows in the old building, a silhouette of an individual was sighted. There were a few gasps and exclamations heard among the walkers, which brought a chuckle from Lee.

"That's just a dummy. We put it there to scare the scouts," he said, referring to the periodic visits by girl scouts from across the nature to the Girl Scout headquarters, the old Lowe House.

GHOST TOUR GUIDE HAS HAD HAUNTING EXPERIECES

Ghosts are hot commodities to "A Haunting Experience" tour guide/manager Pallas, who banks highly on the existence of ghosts in St. Augustine. It's his business to convince people there are some creepy things going on around the old town. "A Ghostly Experience," features walking tours, riding tours and sailing tours, all of which promise to bring thrills to the viewer.

In the summer of 2005, Pallas joined the "A Ghostly Experience" tour operation as manager. Long before becoming a ghost tour guide, Pallas said he had had a paranormal experience.

He recalled was sitting in an old tavern in Connecticutt "just relaxing and drinking some beer with some friends." Suddenly, he recalled, a frigid blast of air swept over him. "It was like someone had turned an air conditioner on high and aimed it directly at me."

He spoke to the tavern owner about it and was told, "Yeah, it happens all the time."

"But what is it that happens?" Pallas asked.

"We aren't sure what that guy is up to," was the tavern owner's reply.

Upon more prodding, Pallas was informed that it seemed to be a resident ghost who appeared with his cold blast from time to time.

Pallas says his wife is much more sensitive to the paranormal than he is, but says he has seen the St. Augustine Lighthouse ghost several times. In fact, he has seen more than one ghost on the Lighthouse property, he says.

TAPS, a renowned paranormal research and investigations group that does paranormal investigations in various parts of the country to confirm or dispel rumors of haunted places, examined the lighthouse. In a televised broadcast, investigators encountered enough activity and caught enough sights and sounds on their cameras to declare it "definitely haunted."

The Shadow Behind You--

The lighthouse, located across the Lions Bridge on St. Augustine Beach, dates back to the 1500's when it guided Sir Francis Drake onto the coast of St. Augustine. His men pillaged what they could and burned to the ground both the nearby settlement and the

The Shadow Behind You--

tower. Historical records indicate the old tower was rebuilt many times and finally, was partly replaced by a coquina structure, topped by the wooden tower. It succumbed to the elements after surviving the Revolution War. Through all these years, a Spanish soldier stood guard at the lighthouse, which was actually a lookout tower during the war.

History notes a tragedy when Joseph Andreau was painting the tower. His scaffolding failed and the plunged to his death.

The Civil War came and went past the old lighthouse, which by this time was dark, having been neglected for too many years.

On October 15, 1874, under the supervision of Hezekiah H. Pittee, a new lighthouse was completed and the lamp once again was illuminating, but it had taken many years, much hard work and heart ache to make it become a reality.

Although the lighthouse site has witnessed several deaths, and is said to be housed by spirits of this stormy past, it is the Pittee family that Pallas remembers best of those connected to the lighthouse's dark history.

Hezekiah H. Pittee brought his family to St. Augustine while he supervised the construction of the tower. He had three daughters who played on the grounds around the lighthouse. The construction site used a railway track to move supplies from the pier and one day, the three daughters, along with the child of one of the construction workers, were riding the cart, when it ran off the end of the track and into the water. Two of Pittee's daughters, Mary and Elizabeth, along with the daughter of the worker, perished that day.

Pallas weaves this historical yarn and warns his tour goers that they might see movement of the swings that hang beneath the bent and twisted live oaks that grace the lighthouse grounds. Either Elizabeth or Mary appears regularly at the lighthouse and Pallas said he has seen the apparition several times. She usually is swinging on the swings in the yard of the former Pittee house, which is now the site of the Lighthouse Museum., Pallas says.

Pallas is so certain the ghosts seen there could be either Mary or Elizabeth, because the time frame fits either of the two girls. He said he has seen her in different forms: shoulder and head, but never full figure. This scenario seems to be backed up by the TAPS visit, when the investigators saw a partial form of a lady on the lighthouse property.

Sometimes, says Pallas, it is just the essence of a person swinging on the swing, when it sways back and forth without benefit of a wind.

Part of his ghost tour vernacular included reports of a figure seen on one of the light house levels, smoking a pipe. It has been theorized, Pallas said, that the apparition might have been a former lighthouse keeper who often stepped out on the balcony for a smoke.

TAPS investigators, during a televised visit to the lighthouse, clearly caught sight of a head and shoulders that appeared to be peering at them from one of the many landings of the structure.

On a dark night in November, some of the tour guests on one of Pallas' "Haunted Express" events were a little playful and slipped over and started the swing swaying back and forth. They spoiled the effect, however, when the perpetrators giggled at their deed.

Pallas took the ribbing good naturedly and assured them they would know the difference between a guest helping the atmosphere along and the real thing.

Dressed all in black, Pallas conducts his tours with a dramatic flair. His deep melodious voice captivates his audience.

"I love to listen to him. He sounds like a preacher," a tour participant commented.

One of Pallas' favorite topics seems to be Henry Flagler and all that he did and did not do for St. Augustine. Although most agree that Henry Flagler, a wealthy tycoon who first visited St. Augustine in 1884 transformed St. Augustine and changed it forever, not everyone likes those changes and not everyone thinks they were made solely for the benefit of the people of St. Augustine.

Pallas called him a greedy man with deep pockets who did not abide by competition. Flagler built the gigantic Hotel Ponce de Leon, which later became Flagler College. Then he built the Alcazar across

King Street from the Ponce de Leon. This hotel is now Lightner Museum.

He paved streets, built businesses and churches, developed a residential section north of his hotels, constructed athletic fields, started a dairy and built a laundry for his hotels.

With all this he still was not loved by everyone. Some thought of him as a selfish, pompous man and many did not want the progress he brought to the city.

Many strange events occurred after his death in 1913.

Passing the old Flagler Hotel, Pallas tells about the rich Henry Flagler and points to the Lightner Museum, which first housed Flagler's Hotel Alcazar and declared, "Guests here have seen ghosts floating around the dining room."

It seems plausible that if ghosts are in this building, a good place to float around is in the current restaurant which is actually operated in the "deep end of the pool." Flagler, with his flair for the opulence, had constructed a huge indoor swimming pool in his hotel, said to cover a city block. Now empty of its many gallons of water, the pool is now the focal point of the popular restaurant.

But, says Pallas, there's a male ghost that stands guard at the entrance of the museum, too.

Sometimes sightings involve energy in the form of streaks or lights as bold as lightning bolts, and sometimes it is merely orbs. Some take on the mystic appearance of a veil or shadow and some are identifiable. Most experiences are as brief as a second or two, Pallas said.

OTHER PLACES, OTHER STORIES

You don't have to visit a city with horse and buggy rides, tour buses and trolleys to find places where people have ghost stories to tell, as has been noted in other the cemetery encounters in rural Manatee County, FL.

While some stories may originate from folks in the tourist business, designed to entertain their clients, many are the product of beliefs by individuals who claim to have had personal encounters, or know someone who has. Whether they're history, folklore, or the over-active imagination, these stories are told by people who sincerely believe they have witnessed a paranormal event.

St. Augustine Innkeeper James is one of those individuals. Although she was a former ghost tour guide, she is no longer in that business, but she says she does recommend tours to her guests of the inn. And she says she is surrounded by spiritual beings in her home.

James says she is constantly encountering the beings that occupy her home, a refurbished cottage dating back a number of years.

"I'm very sensitive to the spirit world," James says. The supernatural she is in touch with in her cottage are not spirits of St. Augustine, but are James' English ancestors, she believes.

Mandy Van Wagenen said she believed a ghost has been living in her apartment. She plans a meal, goes to the market and buys the things she needs then goes to work. Van Wagenen is a waitress at the Gypsy Cab Co. Restaurant on Anastasia Island, across the Lions Bridge from St. Augustine.

"When I get home and start to fix something like macaroni and cheese, I can't find the cheese," she gave as an example.

"Maybe I just have too many beers and can't remember where I put stuff," she said with a chuckle. "But I believe I have a ghost who is hiding that stuff from me."

Van Wagenen is near enough to the St. Augustine lighthouse to perhaps have visits from the spirits said to be housed in and around that imposing structure.

The Shadow Behind You--

Lighthouses may be fertile for the ghost population. Pedro Mendez de Aviles, the 16th century Spanish explorer who was instrumental in the settling of St. Augustine, moved southward after founding the city. He made his way to Jupiter, FL amid wars, with bloody consequences. History has it that the mutiny at Jupiter Inlet may have been Menendez' most vicious battle in his quest to settle Florida. A consequence of the wars in Jupiter was the construction of the Jupiter Lighthouse. Like the lighthouse at St. Augustine, this one was built and destroyed several times, and each time, there was a loss of many lives.

Workers and visitors to the Jupiter Lighthouse have experienced eerie events in and around the facility. Visitors swear they have seen a teenage boy who lights the lamp at night.

Florida, like Georgia, has many sites that believers claim are haunted. And not all of them are historic places, nor are all the buildings old buildings.

C. Stephens, is a Florida nurse, believes the hospital in which she works is haunted. She said several patients in the hospital swear they have seen a male ghost there, and some claim to have been pushed hard enough by the ghost to make them fall. There have been tales from patients of apparitions walking outside on the window ledge, and tapping on the windows of hospital patient rooms. This 40-year old hospital, like all hospitals, has seen its share of death, suffering and sadness.

Stephens believes the hospital ghost may have followed her home one night, where he remained for a few days visit.

Famous for turning on lights in unoccupied units of the hospital, the ghost was a natural suspect when Thomas went home from work to find every light in her house on, even though she had turned them all off before leaving.

"This happened several times," Stephens reports. She was planning to have a heart-to-heart talk with the unnamed specter to reach an understanding that if he stays in her house, he should behave himself, but before she got the opportunity, he seemed to have moved

The Shadow Behind You--

on, because the strange events halted at both her home and the hospital.

Paranormal events seemed to come and go in the hospital. There was a time when there was no activity at all, but this soon changed and once again the apparitions were spotted in various parts of the hospital.

Ghost experts, such as Harry Stafford, say this is a normal occurrence. Spirits are not always active.

J. Long, formerly of New York and Miami, FL, now lives in Sarasota, FL. He says he doesn't know if he believes in ghosts or not, but added that he did have a couple of strange, unexplained events to tell about.

"My wife and I had had a disagreement and I went for a walk," he remembers. He said he was walking along muttering aloud to himself about the different approaches his mother and mother-in-law had in raising their children.

"I was really ticked off and mumbled to myself that if my wife's mother had taught her the same things my mother had taught me, we would not have had the disagreement at all and I wouldn't be walking off my anger."

Then, he said, "Something kicked me right in the rear. Honest. I turned around to see who was behind me and no one was there."

He surmised, half in jest, that his deceased mother-in-law probably had taken umbrage to his mutterings and kicked him in the rear.

"This really happened. Somebody kicked me," he insisted.

Another time, Long was waiting to cross a busy street and was about to step onto the pavement, thinking he could get across between cars.

"I could not move. I mean something had hold of me and I was not able to get off that sidewalk," he recalled. It was a good thing, too, because at that moment, a car that had been unseen zoomed past him.

"Something saved my life, that day," he declares.

C. Banner said she had had an encounter with her father in her home in Bradenton, FL. And he had never been in that home, which seems to belie the thought that ghosts don't stray far from their original home. She was going from the bedroom to the bathroom one evening and "I got to a point where I felt I had to pass through my father to get there. His presence was so strong, it was unmistakable," she said.

She went on to say her daughter told her years after an event happened to her, that she, too, had seen her grandfather.

"She loved to sit in my closet and play with her dolls," Banner explained. "All of a sudden, she stopped going into my room at all, unless I was there and it wasn't until just recently that she told me she had been afraid to go there alone, after encountering the ghost of her grandfather."

Banner also had another experience in another state. She and some friends were standing outside a historical mansion and a little girl approached her. "She asked me to play ball with her, so we tossed the ball back and forth for a bit."

Then, she said, she noted some strange looks on her friends' faces. They wanted to know exactly what she was doing.

"When I explained to them I was playing ball with the little girl, they thought I'd lost my mind. They didn't see a little girl at all," she remembered.

"Yes, indeed, I believe in ghosts," she concludes.

Ron Fly, resident artist at the Apple Tree Gallery in Gatlinburg, TN is convinced there are miracles happening every day and he is likewise convinced he had a visit from his great grandfather who had been dead most of Ron's life.

He had done some restoration on a room in his great-grandfather's farmhouse and wanted to paint it as he imagined it would have been with his great grandfather sitting at a desk in the study.

Using the same piece of furniture that he thought had been in the room over the generations, he was doing a self-portrait to use as a

The Shadow Behind You--

Apparently not all ghosts are kind souls. There may be a few demons scattered throughout the ghost community.

C. North has contended for years that she encountered a vicious demon who stayed in her house for months. He tormented her and made her believe she was having a nervous breakdown.

"I really thought I was losing my mind," she said.

Through her ordeal she became very spiritual and believed she had a special pathway to God.

"One night I awoke and it felt like someone had cut off all my air. I thought I was being suffocated to death," she said with tears in her eyes.

"I just knew I was going to die," she recounted.

Then, she somehow found the strength to sit up in bed and shout, "In the name of Jesus Christ," and the feeling went away.

She battled with her own personal demon for almost a year, but he finally seemed to have been brought under control "by the Lord's help," she says.

There is a report of a couple who spent a night in a St. Augustine inn and had a similar experience. They, too, called upon the name of Jesus, and spent the night reciting scriptures from the Bible in order to stop their "demon" from choking the two of them.

Ghost history? Or over-active imaginations? Identical incidents happening to separate people who never met each other? Hmmm.

Ralph Denham says he is not sure but what he had a visitor from the spirit world. He and his wife traditionally take a mid-day snooze. On one of these days, he arose and went into his kitchen where he found a newspaper clipping from England that had an article in it about a long-deceased relative of his wife. He was puzzled as to who entered his house and left the material on his kitchen counter. Calling relatives and friends in the area, he learned that no one took credit for the deed.

"I just cannot imagine who did that," Denham said. "I think it was a ghost," he added in all seriousness.

DISBELIEVERS HAVE THEIR SAY

And then there are those who have definitely made their minds up. They firmly believe there is no such thing as the supernatural.

David Nolan, a St. Augustine renown historian, believes most of the "ghost" stories around St. Augustine are pure poppycock. He says ghost stories are the product of an overactive imagination. And he has history to back up his theory, he says.

"We are just overrun with ghost tours," Nolan said. He added, "Every time you see a cluster of people, more tall tales are being told."

The historian said he believes the tours detract from the "serious history here."

"Just check the public records and you'll see there is simply no truth to most of the stories heard about ghosts in St. Augustine," he said. "Furthermore, there is a lot of misrepresentation on the history of St. Augustine."

Nolan, originally from Boston, has lived in St. Augustine more than 30 years. He worked in the civil rights movement, helped do the government survey of old buildings in St. Augustine, has been active in the Historical Society and has written a book, "The Houses of St. Augustine."

The 1970's government survey was the first official survey of the old buildings in Florida's oldest city.. It was the first official survey of the old buildings. The job entailed maps and directories and dating the old buildings, a task that proved difficult for some of the buildings, because so many had been torn down and rebuilt.

He said he took the government job because when he moved his family to St. Augustine, he had planned to stay home and write a book. He had some savings and thought he could spend a bit of time before he took a job.

"I didn't reckon with inflation, though," he said. "Less than a year later, I found I needed a job to support my family and as it turned out, the Historic Preservation Board was looking for someone to work on a survey of the old buildings," Nolan explained.

The Shadow Behind You--

He was interested in historic buildings, so the job was a nice fit, he said.

While doing the survey, which required him to stand before the houses and make notes, he was sometimes accosted by residents who thought he was with the tax assessors office and was about to take information to the county that would raise their taxes.

"I did some quick explaining that I wasn't with the tax assessor at all," he said with a chuckle.

Many of the "so-called" old buildings on St. George were built within the past 50 years, Nolan claims, adding that the Old School House on St. George is one of the few original buildings remaining. Most of the original buildings along the famed St. George Street were torn down "within my lifetime and rebuilt," Nolan says.

Of all the houses in St, Augustine, only 30 or 35 are true colonial buildings.

"This was history in the making, but some of the folks I met who lived in the houses weren't interested in authenticating their historical value. They were interested in proving their house had a ghost living in it.

"I recall a lady who was about to open a bed and breakfast who asked for help in getting the historic facts about the building.

Nolan directed her to old city directories and showed her how to trace the house and its residents.

"She didn't look five minutes before she informed me 'this is too much work.'" She said she just needed a good ghost story to tell about her place," Nolan recalled.

Nolan said Sandy Craig first started telling ghost stories in the 1990's and started offering tours. When people heard she was telling ghost stories, they started sharing stories with her and "she got more than she could shake a stick at," Nolan remembers.

As Sandy grew more successful with her ghost tours, others joined in and today, "Everybody wants a piece of the action. They all want to make money on the ghosts," he remarked.

They all have a story to tell about a ghost that lives somewhere and none of them can be confirmed by history," Nolan said.

The Shadow Behind You--

He tells about a beautiful Victorian house that became popular with the Flagler College students who were intrigued with tales of the ghost who supposedly lived there. The owner had cut it up and made apartments out of it and rented them to the students. She started telling about the "old sea captain" who built the house, who was a ghostly resident there. She told the students that the house was the only one to survive the fire of 1879. Historically, the original owner of the house was a naval general, not an old sea captain, Nolan claims. He said the reputation of the "old sea captain" was less than perfect and he felt it was a smear on the naval general who actually was the house owner.

"I was constantly being visited by excited students who wanted information on the old sea captain that had lived in the house," he recalled.

"I told them, over and over, that the story was false and no such person lived there."

Nolan said he gets frustrated when the owners of the old houses make no effort to restore them. They do no research on them. They just open them up and tell stories about them. And he gets frustrated over all the tales about supernatural beings inhabiting those houses.

"There's not one shred of proof that any of those stories are true," he said.

He wrote "Houses of St. Augustine" 10 years ago. The book, teeming with old and current photographs, is based on true historical facts about the old homes. Among houses featured in his book are the three oldest houses in St. Augustine. On St. Francis Street sits the "oldest house in the United States," while a house on Aviles Street is a post-Civil War house which was owned during much of the 19th century by free blacks.

It was finally determined by the St. Augustine Historical Society that the oldest house is the old Dodge House on St. George Street, records indicate.

St. Augustine, the scene of many battles, was developed in three stages, Nolan says. Gen. Oglethorpe, of Savannah fame, "lusted for St. Augustine" he added, but failed to gain possession of it when he was defeated in battle. The first settlement dated back many centuries. Then it was reborn in 1880's when Henry Flagler put his railroad through. Then again, in 1920, it had another rebirth during the land boom.

"St. Augustine is the oldest city and people should treasure its buildings and history and not make up fake stories about it," Nolan said.

Although Nolan is anti-ghost stories, tours and beliefs, he admitted the tour faze has done one thing for St Augustine. It's given the city a night life.

"Everyone used to say the sidewalks were rolled up at dark around here. Boy, there's sure a night life now. Every night you can see a cluster of people on the streets. And you can be assured that it's a ghost tour," he explained.

George Koutelas, who works for one of St. Augustine's tour businesses, Sugar Mill Sightseeing Trains, says he's lived in the old Florida town for 67 years and has yet to see a single ghost.

"We never even thought about ghosts until somebody went down to Key West and saw what a big tourist thing they were there and came back here and started one in St. Augustine," he said, adding "now there are at least 20 of them running around after dark all over town."

J. Donaldson, who lives in Dunedin, FL and has spent her life in the south, is a flat "non-believer."

"No way, no how, no time am I believing in ghosts," she states emphatically.

"But I believe in Guardian Angels," she adds. And she also believes there are some people who just have an evil spirit living in them.

"But ghosts? No way."

RESERVED OPINIONS

Many people, like Harry Metz, a historian and guide at the St. Augustine Old Village, leave the door open to their belief in the supernatural.

"I don't really believe in ghosts, but I don't disbelieve, either," he said. A retired airline pilot, he has seen enough strange events to be open minded about their origin.

Some just never thought about it before. Don and Eva Ring are two who fit this category.

"Gee, I don't know what I believe about the paranormal," Eva commented.

"I just never thought too much about it," added Don.

K. Matherson is included in this section of folks with reserved opinions not because he doesn't have an opinion, but that his actions defy what he claims is his opinion.

He said he thinks folks make of things what they want to make of them.

"If people think they are seeing or hearing paranormal activity, then their imagination may well conjure up a supernatural experience."

"An over active imagination can do a lot of things," he added.

But on the other hand, Materson tells the story about his father, who while fighting during World War I in tunnels, becoming buried in one, when it collapsed on him, due to an enemy detonation.

"My dad always said he saw his mother that time in that tunnel, and she helped him escape to freedom," Matherson said. His father's mother had been dead for many years.

History? Or Folklore? Like stories originating from Savannah, St. Augustine, New Orleans, Key West or any of the other reportedly haunted towns in the USA, or the World, the answer remains elusive and depends on the opinions of the person answering the question.

QUESTIONS REMAIN

There are so many unanswered questions about the subject of the paranormal that they may never be answered.

One question asked by both the believer and the non-believer is why now? Why is there so much information about haunted places? Why is it that so many people have lived to be old and have never had a paranormal incidence?

Is it because there is a war being waged against Christianity, as some have said? Is it because folks are opening their minds now to the possibility there are unexplained things out there? Or is it simply because there are more communications now that give folks courage to talk about something they always knew?

Individuals who have had a change of heart in their beliefs in the paranormal ask questions about what they are seeing.

"Why is there a difference in the size of the orbs I have photographed?" asks Barry Miller.

"And what is the significance in the different colors of the orbs?"

Since photographs shown in this book have been in black and white, it is not apparent that different orbs appear to be different colors. Reds, blues, and yellows are often photographed. Some shades of lavender also show up sometimes as do greens.

"Why is that?" Miller wonders.

And why is it that some nights you go to a site and catch not so much as a single orb, and on other nights, there are hundreds hovering around? Miller also asks.

How about you? What do you think about these subject? Do you think these stories are history, or folklore? Are they just things people have made up to cause a tingle up and down your spine with a scary story? Do these people simply have an over-active imagination? Is there a logical explanation for each of these events? Or are they the truth?

You be the judge.

ISBN 141209859-9